Exploring Borders

In *Exploring Borders* Giuseppe Mantovani highlights and explores the ways in which culture acts as a framework organizing our experience. He emphasizes the differences across and between cultures and examines the depths to which these can go. He also analyses the functions of culture, including: mediation, meaning-making and forming a repertory of values and principles. Finally, he considers some of the challenges raised by taking a cultural perspective and examines how these may be addressed in society.

This highly original and eminently readable narrative will be invaluable to scholars of psychology, media and cultural studies, and to all those fascinated by culture and eager to make the cultural dimension visible to all.

Giuseppe Mantovani is Professor of Attitudes at the University of Padova, Italy. His previous publications include *New Communication Environments* (Taylor & Francis).

Exploring Borders

Understanding culture and psychology

Giuseppe Mantovani

London and Philadelphia

First published 2000 by Routledge
11 New Fetter Lane, London EC4P 4EE

Simultaneously published in the USA and Canada
by Taylor & Francis Inc.
325 Chestnut Street, Suite 800, Philadelphia, PA19106

Routledge is an imprint of the Taylor & Francis Group

© 2000 Giuseppe Mantovani

Originally published in 1998 as *L'elefante invisibile – Percorsi di
psicologia culturale* by Giunti Gruppo Editoriale, Villa La Loggia,
via Bolognese 165, 50139 Firenze, Italy

Typeset in Sabon by RefineCatch Ltd, Bungay, Suffolk
Printed and bound in Great Britain by
Biddles Ltd, www.biddles.co.uk

British Library Cataloguing in Publication Data
A catalogue record for this book is available from the British Library

Library of Congress Cataloging in Publication Data
Mantovani, Giuseppe, 1942–
    Exploring borders: understanding culture and psychology/
    Giuseppe Mantovani.
       p. cm.
    Includes bibliographical references and index.
    ISBN 0–415–23100–0 (HB)
       1. Culture. 2. Ethnopsychology. 3. Cultural relativism.
       4. Ethnocentrism. I. Title.
    GN357 .M36 2000
    155.8′2—dc21
                                                    99–087219

ISBN 0–415–23100–0 (hbk)
ISBN 0–415–23400–X (pbk)

Contents

Foreword

I first learned of the work of Giuseppe Mantovani when he sent me a copy of his previous book, *New Communication Environments: From Everyday to Virtual*. Unexpectedly, from Italy, I encountered an exciting book that spoke directly to my interest in communication theories of mind. It placed artifact mediation at the heart of human communication, a process that occurs between people; in so far as human psychological processes are mediated through such artifacts, mind, as conventionally understood, must be seen as distributed across individuals, their human-built environments (their cultures), and their social groups. The quality of human experience depends crucially on what tools are ready to hand, and which can be created along life's way.

The focus of *New Communications Environments* was on how to think about the changes in quality of human experience associated with contemporary digitalized telecommunication systems, a problem of great importance to the discipline of Communication. The present book is informed by Mantovani's theory of how the human mind is conditioned by the media which help to constitute it. But *Exploring Borders* shifts focus. Mantovani's goal in this book is to get us to "remediate" the way we think about culture's role in constituting us as a person. He wants us to apply this new perspective to the urgent need for human beings to accommodate to/with "the other" in order to eradicate the plague of violence that has broken out in the post-Cold War world.

I have worked in the area of culture and human development for most of my professional life, so I am no stranger to the issues that Professor Mantovani discusses here. Many of the examples he gives to illustrate the principles of his approach are also a part of my tool kit for theorizing about the relation of culture and mind. Images such as Kenneth Burke's description of life as like a cocktail party conversation, Jorge Luis Borge's fantastical concoction of an exotic category system (which Mantovani shows is not so fantastical after all, or not in the way we thought it was) or the ubiquitous blind man and his stick, all serve for me as touchstones through which I recognize theorists who adopt a mediational theory of mind.

What astonished me in the present book are the fascinating and carefully chosen examples Professor Mantovani draws upon so artfully that seemingly arcane academic discussions take on a coherent immediacy as we face the difficult question of how to achieve a world in which cultural difference does not mean cultural domination. How might we, Mantovani asks us, achieve a world in which "cultural identity is not a treasure to be jealously defended but an asset to be exchanged openhandedly"?

This is not just a theoretical issue. Recently the President of the United States returned from a trip to the Balkans, where, in the name of humanity, the Anglophone world took the lead in seeking to settle regional ethnic conflicts through force. He told the Albanian people of Kosovo, returned to their homes by virtue of the massive application of force, to stop killing the Gypsies and Serbs who had been killing and robbing them a few months earlier. But the killing and destruction have not stopped. He reminded them of children in Sierra Leone with their hands cut off because they were of the "other" ethnic group and of a girl blinded by flying glass in a bomb blast in Northern Ireland. In both places, he said, the killing has stopped (he may well be proven wrong before these words go to print!). But in Kosovo, in Kurdistan, in Chechnya, in Tibet, in Sri Lanka, and so on, there is no end to such violence in sight, no *Pax Mundi*, if the past is to be our guide.

What is it about human beings that makes them such efficient killers of their own kind? If culture is constitutive of the way people come to understand, desire, and behave in the world, what is culture's role in our ways of experiencing ourselves, and reciprocally, the other? Why does it foster and channel hatred so effectively? This is not just a practically urgent issue, it is an academically urgent issue, because it restates, in highly accessible and varied forms, the same theory of mediation that underpinned Professor Mantovani's earlier work on the new media. Same theory, different focus.

I do not want to diminish readers' pleasure in discovering for themselves the artful way in which Professor Mantovani weaves his story; the variations on his theme of cultural variation as a human resource, not just a threat. For an American reader, this book provides a salutary reminder of our own recent past and serves as an awkward but jolting illustration of academic principles that provide us no such jolt when we are reading about events long ago and far away.

By his own theory, Professor Mantovani knows that this book is but part of a larger dialogue, the "cocktail party of life". He has done both specialists and any interested citizen a favour by reminding us that every encounter with others is two-sided and that we are all blind to crucial parts of the experiences we participate in creating. I hope that other Anglophone readers will enjoy this humane voice from Italy by a scholar who never loses his sense of humour despite the often grim nature of the matters about which he writes.

Mike Cole
University of California, San Diego

Acknowledgements

I would like to thank all those friends, colleagues and students who share my interest in cultural psychology. I am especially grateful to Phil Agre, Jerome Bruner, Dora Capozza, Antonella Carassa, Alan Costall, Bill Clancey, Mike Cole, Kenneth Gergen, Paolo Inghilleri, Richard Lazarus, Olga Liverta, Pino Mininni, Giuseppe Riva, Barbara Rogoff, Eugenia Scabini and Cristina Zucchermaglio. Special thanks go to my friend Gabriel Walton, whose sparkle and humour again shine through this translation, which has been the object of her tender caring.

Introduction

This book deals with the cultural dimension. Culture is something that Western societies have not yet clearly understood, so that the challenges they have to face in an increasingly multi-cultural world are particularly difficult to manage. Understanding culture is certainly not only a Western problem but a universal problem as well, but as Western societies have a position of preeminence in the processes of globalization they have also a special responsibility in acknowledging cultural differences and promoting mutual respect. The first challenge is that launched by the large-scale – indeed, planet-wide – migrations of people who no longer accept giving up their traditions in order to assimilate those of their new host countries. The second challenge is that created by the dissolution of traditional models of Western societies, amplified by the powerful influence of both media and globalization processes: when remote territories are incorporated in an empire, also the customs, tastes and values of the capital are subject to profound change.

The Sakuntala of Kalidasi, famous in Sanskrit literature, tells the story of an elephant standing in front of a meditating sage. The man looks at the animal and says: "That is *not* an elephant". Shortly afterwards, the elephant turns round and begins to move slowly away, while the sage wonders whether there might be an elephant nearby. The elephant finally disappears. At this point the sage declares: "There *was* an elephant here". The story is told by Jerome Bruner (1990), a famous cognitive psychologist, who heard it from an Israeli friend; it was later taken up by Clifford Geertz (1995), an equally famous cultural anthropologist: this bright chain of cultural transmission reaches us as the last link.

The invisible elephant, for us, is the cultural dimension which is so large that it fills our entire visual field and yet remains as elusive as a dragonfly. It is not just that our understanding usually occurs *a posteriori*, stemming from the traces which events, like the invisible elephant of the story, leave behind them. We have trouble in seeing the cultural dimension for the same reason that a fish does not see the water in which it swims. We do not focus on it, we take it for granted because we are constantly immersed in it. Until now, Western culture has been considered by its members not as a peculiar conceptual grid, but as an unquestionable source of objective truth and universal moral principles.

Like the elephant, the cultural dimension really *is* invisible to those who are not prepared to recognize it, although it looms large in the view of those who know what to search for. In fact, culture is not just the elephant, the massive system of practices and symbols which maintain a given society. It is also the dragonfly which flits its transparent wings to accompany the tiny details of everyday life: a tit-bit of gossip about a friend, a witty joke, the use of a metaphor in a newspaper headline. It is the two-sided characteristic of culture which makes it elusive to us. If we consider only one of its two faces, the elephant and the dragonfly, our overall view is incomplete. We must try to see both sides at the same time: order and variation, the solid social fabric and the graceful ballet of improvization.

Our pathway in the cultural dimension passes through four steps. The first, which forms the first part of this book, presents culture as a framework organizing our experiences. All individual cognitive activity comes under its influence: empirical data and traditional beliefs cannot clearly be separated. By means of categorization, the construction of analogies, and recourse to metaphors, culture informs both judgement and prejudice. There is in fact no purely cognitive criterion to distinguish one from the other, since the key difference between the two is based on recognition and acceptance of other people's (and one's own) identity. The ceremony of "taking possession" of the New World told by Christopher Columbus in his letters clarifies this point, as we will see in Chapter 2.

We have used the word *"culture"*, but we should more properly use the plural, *cultures*. The second part of this book examines the depth of cultural differences. Once, Westerners were not disturbed too greatly by differences they saw because they believed that their own system of values was the best and naturally remained anchored to it. Now, when this anchoring system has been weakened, the emergence of radical differences between and among cultures becomes disconcerting. How can one act in a world which, in spite of the fact that it gives a superficial observer the impression of steadily increasing homogeneity, does not in fact march towards assimilation but towards differentiation? There are only two possible paths. One is that followed by Cabeza de Vaca, a Spanish *conquistador* who, after setting off in the sixteenth century from his native land to conquer the New World, became a shaman among the American Indians. He travelled for seven years, from the marshes of Florida to the shores of the Pacific, in the company of his new Indian friends who had accepted him as a respected member of their culture. The other path is that of Daniel Defoe's hero, the stubborn Robinson Crusoe who, with the help of the physical and intellectual tools provided him by his native Puritan culture, colonized his wild tropical island without changing his mind about very much.

The third part of this book analyses the three functions of culture. Cultural psychology has stressed the function of mediation, which is of prime importance, but there are two other functions which cannot be ignored. One is that of producing meaning: by means of a dense network of analogies, culture links different domains of reality and gives all its elements a definite meaning. Another function, which has been relatively poorly studied by the social sciences, is that of forming a repertory of values and principles which deserve respect even when they turn out to be difficult to apply. Every culture teaches its members what is decent, what is worth wishing for, what dignity is. The existence of a repertory of principles allows people to act according to socially recognizable and communicable aims.

The fourth part of this work considers some of the challenges we shall have to face in the near future. What does the cultural perspective suggest? One indication is of "nourishing our ancestors", as Sperber (1974) says, meaning that we should not neglect or forget our history, even when it contains painful or shameful episodes. We have to reflect over it and come to a better understanding of our past, which is still living in our heads and in our environments. Memories are to be cultivated and duly criticized, so that the errors and horrors of the past can be banished from the present. In order for a culture to be transmitted, it is not enough for someone just to tell a story; there must also be someone who listens to it and works on it. A second suggestion deals with education – crucial at this time when we have to choose between the cultural and informational views of education. The latter dominates mass media, which often simply publicize the utopian promises of computer companies. A third suggestion is to keep open spaces for personal reflection, free from the informational overload with which the new electronic technologies burden our minds daily. Information is not knowledge; knowledge is a personal adventure rooted in tradition, continuously subverting it.

I present here an image of culture quite different from the currently accepted one, in which culture is a mould which renders everyone the same. I have also abandoned the idea that Western culture represents the acme of development for human societies. This book, which continues a previous discourse on culture in communication (Mantovani, 1996a), is for people interested in new frameworks for understanding society, cognition and education. Its foundations in cultural psychology, cognitive anthropology and social psychology are examined in the Notes at the end, in which I acknowledge with pleasure our debts to the innovative ideas of Mike Cole, Richard Shweder, and Kenneth Gergen which inspired my work.

The narrative style adopted here aims at favouring sensemaking by readers and also at evoking the experiences of "other" cultures which incessantly enter our discourse because we come to know ourselves mainly through "others". The "others" exemplified here are often the Indians of the Americas before Columbus because we see the "conquest" of the New

World as an emblematic and unique experience: the encounter between two cultures which had remained completely separate until the moment of their dramatic meeting. Ample recourse is made to quotations from other works, in order to place readers as close as possible to the events described: culture is a tradition, the telling of a story, and this book aims to take on the form as well as the content of the cultural transmission. The relationships among diverse cultures are a tangled mix of encounter, confrontation, destruction and, sometimes, unexpected friendship and reciprocal respect. The choice to allow the eye-witnesses of cultural encounters to talk to us stems from the aim of this work, which is that of presenting the cultural dimension as cognitively and morally not neutral.

Part I

Frames of experience

In Boston, a dignitary of the Roman Catholic Church was driving along a lonesome road on the outskirts of the city. Seeing a small Negro boy trudging along, the dignitary told his chauffeur to stop and give the boy a lift. Seated together in the back of the limousine, the cleric, to make conversation, asked, 'Little boy, are you a Catholic?' Wide-eyed with alarm, the boy replied, 'No sir, it's bad enough being colored without being one of those things'

(Allport, 1954: 4)

Who would have thought of finding such a neat little story at the beginning of Allport's celebrated volume on prejudice? It shows us that prejudice spreads its tentacles in all directions. Racial prejudice, deep-rooted in the history of the United States, mingles here with religious prejudice, deep-rooted in the Puritan origins of the noble city of Boston. The black boy feared he would notch up yet another black mark against himself – that of being a Catholic.

The story is set in Boston and anyone who knows the story of that city can easily understand it. Even the boy's terror of finding himself trapped in the incomprehensible quarrels of whites who travel around by limousine is comprehensible. This same story could hardly have been set in Paris. Not because everyone in Paris loves Catholics, but because the stereotypes we expect to find in Gay Paree are different from those supposedly thriving in Boston. But why are people's attitudes so different? How can a cultural environment influence the attitudes of its members to such an extent? We shall see in the following pages.

Chapter 1, *Birds and spirits*, shows how people's experience is structured by a system of categories which has its roots in culture: the Dyirbal aborigines of Australia do not put birds in the same category as animals because, according to their traditional beliefs, birds are the spirits of dead women. Every society supplies its members with a set of beliefs which direct both the judgements and the prejudices of those same members. If we cannot draw a precise line between judgement and prejudice, how can we recognize the latter?

Chapter 2, *The roots of prejudice*, suggests that prejudice consists in denying the cultural identity of other people we meet, as Columbus did during his first voyage of discovery to the Americas in the ritual of "taking possession" of the new lands on behalf of the crown of Spain. Contempt for others and justification for destroying them along with their culture stem from recognizing only one legitimate, rightful, rational way of viewing reality – our own.

Chapter 3, *Metaphors and analogies*, discusses how culture influences our decisions by means of the metaphors we use to frame controversial problems. Problem-solving depends on the way in which problems are posed inside a given culture: every judgement contains elements of prejudice. If we become aware of the intrinsic limitations of our act of judgement, we can accept that our way of seeing things is not necessarily either the only or the best way and that other people are entitled to develop their own ways of organizing their experience.

Chapter 1

Birds and spirits

THE POWER OF CATEGORIES

The Bible tells us that God created all sorts of animals, the birds of the heavens and the wild beasts of the earth, and that he brought them before Adam to find out what he wished to call them. God seems to have been curious to know the names Adam would give animals. His curiosity was justified, because it is precisely through the assignation of names and their groupings into categories that human beings try to order their physical, mental and social world.

Let us imagine that, during that earliest meeting, the animals heard themselves called by name for the first time: *dog, cat, horse, wolf, fox, lynx*, and so on. And then Adam said: "The first three animals are 'good', I consider them as friends and will treat them as such; but the last three are 'bad' for me and I will chase and even kill them whenever I get the chance." Some of the rejected animals would have felt bad about this, they would perhaps have called in the prehistoric equivalent of the Society for the Prevention of Cruelty to Animals, but they would at least have been warned about Adam's intentions towards them.

I too would like to know how the present I gave Anna for her birthday was classified. I gave her a copy of one of my favourite books, Salinger's *The Catcher in the Rye*, but I still don't know whether she liked it, or whether she was offended, considering it to be an allusion to our recurrent arguments about her supposed addiction to TV shows. On which physical and mental shelf has she put my gift? Under what label has she catalogued it? Is there a section for "Nice Books" or "Books To Be Read Immediately"? Because that is where I would like to see it. Even better would be to find it in a special section called "Books Donated By Fascinating People". In actual fact, I am a little nettled by the idea that Anna knows a whole crowd of silly people she classifies as "fascinating". We are just good friends, I know, but I would like to be the only person (or almost) on her list.

By classifying my book as "interesting" or "boring", Anna introduces some order into her world. She decides whether to read it at once, or sometime soon, or simply to forget it or throw it away. By assigning my beloved *The Catcher in the Rye* to a certain category, she organizes her physical environment (will it fit into her new backpack or will it be put up high on a distant shelf?), her mental life (she is bound to read it in the evenings instead of compulsively watching TV), her relationship with me (tomorrow she will tell me she liked it more than *Homefront*) and also her self-image (she will say: "I am not stupid, I loved reading your book").

There are of course various types of names. The most specific are individual, like Christian names: "Alice" is that wretched younger sister of mine, always whining round me like a mosquito. "Mark" is that horribly muscular young man Anna has sworn never to see again. "Anna" of course is my best friend (you will probably have realized that already). Apart from proper names, there are other terms – like *book, shelf, jasmine, dream* – which have a wider field of application. And then there are even more general terms, categories, which we use to highlight similarities and differences in those aspects of reality that are relevant to us.

It is important to note that categories organize not only linguistic productions and mental activities but also social reality. For example, words used on the island of Bali to indicate eating – *miunan, maraynam, ngayengang, madaar, ngamah, ngaloklok, neda* and *nyaseksek* – reveal and maintain a strict social hierarchy. The first two words are used for the highest members of the priesthood and nobility. *Ngayengang* is used for the remaining high castes. *Madaar* is used for foreigners, when the status of a person is unclear, or for courtesy, as well as for sick people. *Ngamah* is used for the lowest castes, but serves also for animals in general. There is also a separate hierarchy for animals, reflected in words designating their ways of eating: *ngaloklok* is used for animals which swallow their food, like dogs and pigs; *neda* is reserved for dogs belonging to people of high caste, while *nyaseksek* refers specifically to chickens (Hobart, 1987).

This Balinese categorization combines the human world with the animal one: it tells us that low-caste humans eat like animals, but it also assures us that dogs belonging to high-caste persons have better table manners than ordinary ones. The classification of animals and plants which we in the West studied at school, with Latin names for genera, species and families, is the result of the work of seventeenth-century naturalists, of whom the most renowned was Linnaeus, a Swedish scientist, famous in his own time also for his obstinacy in insisting on placing human beings among the quadrupeds. This opinion caused him to enter into bitter controversy with his colleagues who, strangely enough, were not very pleased at being lumped together with deer, donkeys and pigs – a further example of the social relevance of categorization.

A BIZARRE CATALOGUE

If Anna's mind contained a special section for me, I would feel on top of the world. In fact, I would feel like the Emperor mentioned in the catalogue of animals which Borges (1960) says he found in an ancient Chinese encyclopaedia, "The Celestial Emporium of Benevolent Knowledge", which lists animals in a really curious way:

> (a) those that belong to the Emperor, (b) embalmed ones, (c) those that are trained, (d) suckling pigs, (e) mermaids, (f) fabulous ones, (g) stray dogs, (h) those that are included in this classification, (i) those that tremble as if they were mad, (j) innumerable ones, (k) those drawn with a very fine camel's hair brush, (l) others, (m) those that have just broken a flower vase, (n) those that resemble flies from a distance.
>
> (Borges, 1960: 108)

The Chinese catalogue seems to challenge both logic and common sense – although it is so witty and imaginative that we suspect that Borges himself invented it – because the various categories it contains are mixed, instead of staying clearly separate as they should be. For example, although mermaids fall into category (e), they are also fabulous animals (f), although I personally would hesitate to include among the animals those charming girls I came to know so well last August in a disco down on the Adriatic coast. Mermaids may also belong to the Emperor (a), and be trained (c) like dolphins in an aquarium (the thought makes me shudder), or even embalmed (b) (even more horrible thought). At the idea of being embalmed, the poor mermaids would have good reason to tremble as if they were mad (i) and could be depicted with gooseflesh with the court painter's very fine camel's hair brush (k).

How confusing! Only one case, that of poor mermaids trained and trembling, has destroyed the entire ordering of the animals of the benevolent encyclopaedia. Why make a subdivision which does not really subdivide anything? In actual fact, the mermaids are not the only ones to blame for this. We can think of innumerable other cases of the same kind – that of a suckling pig belonging to the Emperor which has just broken a priceless vase and is trembling for its life, and so on – which would shake the foundations of the delicate architecture of the "Celestial Emporium". And speaking of trembling, it comes to my mind that Anna too trembles like a leaf when she watches a horror film – or does she just pretend, to make me sit closer and put my arm round her for comfort? I really don't know what category to put *her* in.

Borges's list serves our purpose: it reveals the seemingly arbitrary character of many of our forms of organizing knowledge. It shows us that assigning a certain element to a certain category depends heavily on context and on the interpretation we give of the situation in which the element is embedded. I can put Anna in the category of trembling animals only if I believe she really does tremble when watching horror films – otherwise she would have to go in the class of scheming actresses. As for animals "that resemble flies from a distance", they too depend on the interpretation a person gives of what he or she sees. Anna (I'm becoming a little obsessed by the girl, I must admit) does look like a fly if you see her from a long way away zipping down a ski slope; I am afraid that if she knew I am comparing her with a fly, she would not take it at all well. I had better say she executes precise turns on the snow in her smart black ski-suit, moving as elegantly as a dragonfly.

In its strange choices of categories, the Chinese catalogue suggests that our way of ordering the real world is only one of many possible ways – not the only one or even the best one. We do not perceive reality "as it is" but, according to an important branch of social psychology (Gergen, 1994), we construct it by means of our discursive practices. I prefer to use a different metaphor referring to exploration rather than construction of reality – because it may seem a little audacious to say that we create things when in actual fact we usually limit ourselves to the task of ordering them according to our contingent needs. Each of us knows only too well that there are many other things in reality beyond what we manage to catch in our nets.

The metaphor of exploration leaves open the casket of surprises which reality reserves for each of us: in our voyages of discovery, we can always find something more, something different, from our previous expectations. We explore reality by relying on the maps that our culture has given us. We are aware that we need them to venture into wild, unknown lands or cross uncharted seas, but we know also that, accurate though our maps may be, they do not exhaust the multi-faceted possibilities of the real environment we are exploring (Mantovani, 1996a). They only tell us a few things, and approximately at that. Some aspect of reality always escapes us, engrossed as we are in our system of categories and expectations.

People use their more or less incomplete maps to orient themselves with respect to their objectives, which means that the same territory may be mapped in various ways depending on the actor's current interests: Frank's map of the Yukon shows goldfields, because Frank is a gold-digger; Kitty's map shows the carriage routes because she is a dancer in saloons frequented by gold-diggers; and, on his own map, Bill has marked all the waterways where beavers live, because Bill is a hunter of furs.

How do we construct the maps we use to explore the territories of reality? A plausible, commonsense answer is that experience teaches each of us the most suitable categories for ordering our particular world. The subdivision of classes in the apocryphal Chinese catalogue, for example, may appear extravagant to those who, like ourselves, are not the subjects of a despotic Chinese emperor. If we were, the first item on the list would be not at all weird for us; on the contrary, it would be of the utmost importance to us because it would convey a valuable warning: "If you want to avoid trouble, stay away from animals which belong to the Emperor". The experience of disobeying this rule and being duly punished would confirm the wisdom of the "Benevolent Catalogue", which would then no longer appear funny but a useful practical guide for foreigners wishing to pay a visit to the Forbidden City.

TRADITIONAL GRIDS

However, experience is never found in a state of natural innocence, pure and untarnished by previous expectations and traditional beliefs. It develops inside a cultural framework which makes it possible and at the same time constrains it. Experience does teach us how we can proceed in our exploration of the world around us, but it is tradition which states, at the beginning of our journey, what we must experience and how. This is a closed circle: each of us must judge, according to how we appreciate the ineluctable sheet-anchor which holds experience fast to tradition, whether it is a virtuous circle or a vicious one.

If we were to prepare our personal catalogues of animals, we would see the ordering of our own interests reflected in them. A member of the World Wildlife Fund would highlight rare at-risk species; a science teacher would use Linnaeus's taxonomy to give his pupils a systematic vision of the whole; a fearful child would want to know first of all which animals were dangerous and which not. Apart from differences due to peculiar individual interests, all these catalogues would turn out to be relatively similar if they were prepared by people sharing school curricula, religious beliefs, language, country, profession, social status and preferred hobbies. They would be far from similar if we asked people from different countries and cultures to prepare them: as regards food, for example, millions of people throughout the world never touch pork in any shape or form, whereas others have pork barbecues and gnaw spare ribs with gusto; some appreciate as a delicacy a certain grub found in the bark of trees and eaten raw, others shudder at the very idea.

The role of culture in producing categories is highlighted by Lakoff (1987) starting from Dixon's (1982) work on the classification of things according to the Dyirbal, an Australian aboriginal tribe in whose langauge each name must be preceded by one of the following four classificators: *bayi*, *balan*, *balam* or *bala*. If you want to speak Dyirbal corrrectly, you must know exactly which of the four classificators precedes a certain name. The Dyirbal, obviously, have ideas very different from ours about how things are reciprocally connected. We can use their listings in order to understand how categories are produced: sometimes we can have a better view of things which are close to us if we stand back a little to gain a new and better vantage point.

The Dyirbal universe, Lakoff says following Dixon's studies, is divided into four broad categories:

1. the first category, requiring the use of *bayi*, includes "men, kangaroos, possums, bats, most fishes, some birds, most insects, the moon, storms, rainbows, boomerangs, some spears, etc.";
2. the second category, using the classificator *balan*, includes: "women, bandicoots, dogs, platypuses, echidnas, some snakes, some fishes, most birds, fireflies, scorpions, crickets, the hairy mary grub, anything connected with water or fire, sun and stars, shields, some spears, some trees, etc.";
3. the third category, requiring *balam*, includes "all edible fruit and the plants that bear them, tubers, ferns, honey, cigarettes, wine, cake, etc.";
4. the last category, *bala*, applies to "parts of the body, meat, bees, wind, yamsticks, some spears, most trees, grass, mud, stones, noises and language, etc." (Lakoff, 1987: 93).

We seem to have returned to Borges's list in the "Celestial Emporium". For example, the presence of "some spears" in as many as three out of four categories recalls the difficulty of confining our mermaids to a single category. We may wonder at the criteria according to which such very dissimilar beings and objects as women, fireflies, scorpions, sun and stars are put in the same class. A malicious reader might insinuate that certain similarities can be found between women and echidnas, but the poor aboriginal Dyirbal certainly cannot be blamed for such a perverse, badly prejudiced and politically incorrect association.

The Dyirbal categorization does in fact follow a precise logic: the first class basically contains men and animals; the second women, water, fire, and war; the third food which is not meat; and the fourth everything else not found in the other three. The very existence of this residual class, corresponding to "all the others" of Borges's list, is useful because it clears the field of accessory elements and allows us to concentrate on things we consider more important.

In the Dyirbal world, the fact that an object belongs to one of the four classes is established according to whether it resembles other objects in that class or whether it is related to one or more objects typical of it. The affinities linking objects to each other are of various kinds: utensils used for fishing are put together with fish in the first class because they refer to the same sphere of practical activity; plants producing edible fruit are put together with those kinds of fruit in the third class; and the sun and stars fall into the second class, together with fire, from which they take their brilliance.

Although some links may remain obscure to us, for the Dyirbal they are as clear as the relationship – obvious also to us – between fire and sun. A Dyirbal knows very well, for instance, that birds are the spirits of dead women, and they therefore fall in the second class, with other women. That is in fact their proper place: no Dyirbal would dream of putting the spirits of his dead ancestresses among the animals in the first class. The Dyirbal world contains many affinities which we in the West would not suspect and also many differences which we would never imagine.

For example, the yellow wagtail, although a bird, is also the incarnation of a mythical hero and is therefore set in the first class with other men – not with women, or like other birds which, as we have seen, are not listed among animals. The sun and the moon are man and wife, as in the West but, for the Dyirbal, their roles are reversed: the sun is the wife and is therefore placed in the second class with other women, and the moon is the husband, and stays in the first class with the other husbands. In the representation of the celestial bride and groom, fire and splendour belong more to the woman rather than to the man, which many of us would find surprising.

If any conflict arises between the empirical characteristics of an object and the features attributed to that object by tradition, the latter prevails: birds are not animals *because* it is common knowledge that they are spirits. The conflict is resolved before it arises: birds *are* spirits. It is the cultural system which controls what people perceive and believe. There are no objective, independent, empirical data on one hand and opinable, cultural, interpretative constructions on the other: Experience is unitary and is shaped by pre-existing cultural grids (Note 1). When the Dyirbal see a bird, they do not say: "Here is an embarrassing contradiction: this bird looks just like an animal (empirical experience), but tradition demands that we consider it the spirit of a dead woman (cultural belief). How can we get out of this difficulty?" They simply say: "That bird is a spirit". Since they accept the idea that the spirits of women inhabit this world in the form of birds, the Dyirbal do not detect any conflict between experience and tradition in this matter: in the familiar language used to communicate with taboo relatives of the other sex, a single expression, *balan muguyngam*, designates both dead women's spirits and birds.

The attribution of objects to the four classes is automatic, not the result of individual problem-solving or a group decision. It is tradition, not the decision of a single individual or even the advice of elders, which has established that birds are dead women's spirits and that the sun is the wife of the moon. Tradition has established these things according to a system of symbolic correspondences which precedes both individual experience and group discussion.

CULTURE AND PREJUDICE

It is impossible to separate data from interpretation, experierience from discourse (Note 2), observation from cultural framework. In our world too, as among the Dyirbal, myths mould people's experiences, only "our" myths seem to be reasonable or even obvious: girls choose their boyfriends according to stereotypes offered by TV, children in primary school hope to save gorillas from extinction as Diane Fossey does in the film *Gorillas in the Mist*, the *mafiosi* of New York City and Las Vegas copy the gestures of Marlon Brando in *The Godfather*. According to a report from the *Philadelphia Daily News* (in Gergen, 1991), a high school girl withdrew her accusation of rape one month after having made it to the police, and went to live with the man who had raped her, a house painter addicted to drugs, because that was what the heroine of *General Hospital* did in a similar situation and the girl wanted to imitate her. If a television serial can turn a rape into the beginnings of a love story, why should the Dyirbal culture not be able to transform birds into spirits?

When we realize that "normal" judgement is inscribed in an already existing framework, we must re-examine our conception of prejudice (Note 3). As our judgement cannot avoid embodying preconceptions imposed by tradition, prejudice turns out not to be the foolish younger brother of judgement and reason, but simply judgement we cannot accept because it is based on premises so extraneous to our minds that they appear to be absurd. Our culture has often condemned as prejudice the way of thinking of people belonging to societies far removed from our own: "native" remedies for curing diseases, and the ways of treating women, looking after children or venerating gods were denigrated for centuries by European merchants, priests and colonial administrators as forms of ignorance, cruelty and irrationality.

The definition of prejudice as "an avertive or hostile attitude toward a person who belongs to a group, simply because he belongs to that group, and is therefore presumed to have the objectionable qualities ascribed to the group" (Allport, 1954: 18) is hardly acceptable in the light of what we said about categorization. Let us take an example: Richard is totally opposed to drug trafficking (i.e., he has "an avertive or hostile attitude" towards it) and sees a man selling drugs in the street. Before knowing whether the drug pedlar is called Jim or Albert or indeed anything about him ("simply because he belongs to that group" which he does not tolerate), he calls the police and tries to stop the drug seller from continuing his illegitimate business. It is improbable that we would call Richard a victim of prejudice; we would be more likely to say he was acting like a responsible citizen.

The situation would be very different if Richard reacted in a hostile manner whenever he saw a dark-skinned young man wanting a room in his same hotel or whenever he met a Jewish boy coming out of the synagogue on a

Saturday. Why do we approve of Richard's hostility when it is directed towards the drug trafficker but condemn it when it is directed towards a young black boy or a Jew? The difference between the two situations does not lie in the form of Richard's system of beliefs, which may be more or less stereotyped or preconceived, but in their content. His hostility towards the drug trafficker seems to be justified; that towards blacks or Jews repugnant. Why? Clearly because we see things very differently from Richard.

We would say that he has ideas which we judge unacceptable and which we reject whereas social psychologists usually supply another kind of explanation: they say that Richard's hostility towards blacks and Jews is the result of a cognitive error. He is simply making a mistake, he is not reasoning properly. The advantages of this kind of response are obvious: it not only assures us that Richard is wrong in being racist, which is quite comforting; it also indicates how we can cure him of his error. All we have to do is make him use his brain, show him how things really are, help him to free himself from "prejudice", just as we help thick-headed students over abstruse problems in mathematics.

Our cultural perspective maintains that his attitude is first a social and moral fact and then an intellectual and private one. Richard's racist attitude does not stem from the fact that he sees reality in an insufficiently "objective" way – something which is inevitable to a certain extent, as we have seen – but from the fact that his categories of interpretation of reality, his Chinese catalogue, are influenced by the hostility which his community has developed towards particular human groups.

Before being a prejudice, in many countries racism was a religious obligation, a state law, a belief respected and taught to others. African slaves in the southern United States, Jews in Christian countries in medieval and modern Europe, and Armenians in the Turkey of Kemal Ataturk were all discriminated against and persecuted by the highest civil and religious institutions. How can we ignore this painful past? Only by coming into contact with the dark areas of our history can we hope to see the birth, in ourselves and in others, of sentiments different from those produced by a grim past.

Chapter 2

The roots of prejudice

PATHWAYS IN THE WILD

Although the influence of culture in forming people's ideas is easy to see, psychology books speak only of people who have strong or weak prejudices towards blacks, Jews, Puerto Ricans and so on. They constantly refer to individuals, not to communities and cultures, with the result that in the end we cannot understand individuals themselves or make out why they have certain beliefs rather than others. We saw in the previous chapter that people interpret situations by resorting to a repertory of pre-existing categories which are not produced in the recesses of individual minds but are transmitted by the communities in which those individuals began their social lives.

The family, school and church are communities of this type. So are the football team, the dancing class and the Elvis Presley Fan Club – they too may play an important role in the transmission of values: how can we deny that music and songs are capable of suggesting ways of feeling, viewing others, dreaming? The very newspapers we read, the volunteer group we belong to, and the TV programmes we follow every week influence us to a considerable extent. If we ask ourselves how it was that we developed a certain vision of the world, we cannot answer unless we put forward as one of the causes the environment in which we grew up.

The role of culture in our lives derives from the fact that social reality extends far beyond mere interpersonal relationships. Culture establishes bonds between individuals, sets them within a framework; and this framework creates between them special links concerning particular values which are codified in those particular maps which people use to explore reality. In this sense, culture is not something which can be learned: it is the basis for any possible future learning. We do not learn a culture, we enter it. It is not we who acquire culture but culture which acquires us (Bruner, 1993) and allows us to live inside its symbolic order.

The Australian aborigines conceive this order as a network of songs which criss-cross the whole earth in a pattern of paths. Bruce Chatwin (1987) describes the birth of songs on the first morning of the world, when the

Ancestors – the Serpent Man, the Cacatua Man, the Worm Man, the Honeyant – came out of the earth, awakened by the Sun which was rising in the sky for the first time: "The mud fell from their thighs, like placenta from a baby. Then, like the baby's first cry, each Ancestor opened his mouth and called out, 'I AM!' 'I am – Snake . . . Cockatoo . . . Honeyant . . . Honeysuckle . . . And this first 'I am', this primordial act of naming, was held, then and forever after, as the most secret and sacred couplet of the Ancestor's song" (Chatwin, 1987: 73).

All things were encountered, named and sung:

> Each of the Ancients, now basking in the sunlight, put his left foot forward and called out a second name. He put his right foot forward and called out a third name. He named the waterhole, the reedbeds, the gum trees – calling to right and left, calling all things into being and weaving their names into verses. The Ancients sang their way all over the world. They sang the rivers and ranges, salt-pans and sand dunes. They hunted, ate, made love, danced, killed: wherever their tracks led they left a trail of music. They wrapped the whole world in a web of songs.
>
> (Chatwin, 1987: 73)

Everyone, women and men, coming into the world, inherits from their parents a piece of the song of their totemic Ancestors, whether it is the Emu, the Lizard or the Giant Varano, and this song is necessary to find one's way in any part of the country. The pattern of inherited songs is literally a map. The aborigines believe that, by means of appropriate initiations, an individual learns to recognize the link between certain combinations of notes and the movements which the feet of the Ancestors made as they crossed that river or climbed those rocks. The notes of the song and the movement of the feet reproduce the characteristics of the path, terrain and landscape, which are evoked by the song as if they were visible, almost as if we ourselves were following in the footsteps of the Ancestors.

Any person who knows and remembers the song can never lose their way, however far from home they may be. Their home extends over the whole territory which was once trodden by the Ancestor. The descendant may recognize a particular place by starting from that part of the song which describes it. This image of the pathways of song is extremely efficacious in indicating the function of tradition, providing as it does a track which may be followed by those who come after. It suggests that culture – in which individuals find their social roles – recognizes all sorts of individual differences: each person is guided by his peculiar inherited part of the immense web of songlines stretching all over the world. We are not cultural clones; we each have our own songline to follow.

A FATAL MEETING

Differences exist not only inside the same culture, like those between individuals who have received different songs from different Ancestors, but also among cultures. The existence of cultures unlike our own, which structure the lives of their peoples in different ways, is now part and parcel of our daily experience: each of us can have Brazilian neighbours, Korean colleagues and a Chinese take-away on the corner of the street; our friends' country house is rented by a couple of Japanese singers; when we go shopping we encounter women veiled according to Islamic law; and the young man sitting next to us in the train is reading a newspaper printed in Arabic.

Cinema, tourism and the new electronic environments of communication have extended the framework of our experience to faraway cultures. Every evening, we meet the entire world on our TV screens and are encouraged to plan our next holiday to the Caribbean, Mexico or Australia. At certain moments and from certain points of view this is exciting; at others it is disorientating. Trying to cope with the Babel of languages which assail our ears on the streets of any modern city, many of us feel confused, retire into our personal shells, ignore other people or try to avoid them.

Hostility towards others may be directed either towards particular people or groups, or towards the traditions of those other people or groups. The most radical forms of intolerance are those which ignore or discredit the cultural identity, traditions and values of others by taking for granted that the only acceptable system of values is our own and by requiring others to accept it without question. Stephen Greenblatt (1991) has devoted a fascinating book to analysing this type of negation of other cultures during the first contacts of the European explorers with native Americans. He shows how European admiration for the marvels of the New World was rapidly converted into its total destruction.

Columbus's landfall on a Caribbean island on 12 October 1492 was marked by a stupefying singularity: for the first time in Western history, an encounter lacking any pre-existing knowledge occurred. Its impact was not softened by the type of recognitions which until that moment had accompanied Europeans' contacts with other cultures. Both trade contacts, as narrated by Marco Polo, and military conflicts, like the Crusades to the Holy Land, had followed partially worn paths: "Virtually all prior recorded encounters between Europeans and other cultures took place across boundaries that were to some degree, however small, porous; this means that all prior encounters had been to some degree, however small, anticipated" (Greenblatt, 1991: 54).

But that fatal meeting on an autumn day just over 500 years ago between Columbus and the natives was an event without precedent. Let us try to evoke it in our minds, in order to understand how it was that marvel in the face of a new world turned into immediate annihilation. In his famous letter to Luis de Santangel, Columbus begins the account of his first voyage of discovery:

> As I know that you will be pleased at the great victory with which Our Lord has crowned my voyage, I write this to you, from which you will learn how in thirty-three days I passed from the Canary Islands to the Indies with the fleet which the most illustrious king and queen, our sovereigns, gave to me. And there I found very many islands filled with people innumerable, and of them all I have taken possession for their highnesses, by proclamation made and with the royal standard unfurled, and no opposition was offered to me.
>
> (Greenblatt, 1991: 52).

Columbus emphasizes that the rightness of his act was not challenged: "*y no me fué contradicho*". A notary duly recorded the ceremony of taking possession. How could the Arawak Indians, the inhabitants of the island, object to Columbus's claim? The ceremony was carried out by means of a ritual incomprehensible to them, in a language unknown to them, by persons who did not correspond to any figures existing in their world. In their islands, there were neither large wooden ships nor ocean-travelling admirals nor soldiers with steel swords and helmets. Neither were there notaries, certificates or written records. The Arawak, who were probably observing the scene from the edge of a nearby clearing, did not take part in the ritual. They were nobodies in their own land. If they did not say anything it was because they were excluded, beyond the pale.

Why, therefore, did Columbus state that his act of taking possession was not contested? It is very unlikely that he was being ironic about such a delicate matter, on which the hopes of future economic and political fortune for him and his heirs depended. And it is equally improbable that he wished to show a degree of cynicism which would have been completely out of place at such a solemn moment. In Greenblatt's opinion, Columbus's declaration reveals his complete indifference to the other's conscience. For Columbus, at that decisive moment, the other existed only as an empty sign, a zero. The negation of the existence and rights of the native inhabitants arose from the Europeans' greed to appropriate whatever they wanted without parley, without even really recognizing anyone at all.

TAKING POSSESSION

It was not by chance that Columbus's exploring ships carried with them a notary but not a priest, although Columbus attributed an eminently religious aim to his enterprise – he even started signing himself "Christoferens", the bringer of Christ, after his first voyage to the Indies. The presence of a notary who recorded and certified the ritual of taking possession was not an empty formality, but reflected the substance of what was actually happening. "Ceremonies take the place of cultural contracts; rituals of possession stand in for negotiated contracts", Greenblatt says. The ritual was used to remove the natives from the scene and to deny recognition of their rights:

> "There are no attempts in the initial landfall to inscribe the Spanish presence on the land, to leave even an ephemeral mark such as a gash in a tree or a cleared patch of grass. His actions are performed entirely *for a world elsewhere*. For Columbus taking possession is principally the performance of a set of linguistic acts: declaring, witnessing, recording. The actions are public and official: the admiral speaks as a representative of the king and queen, and his speech must be heard and understood by competent, named witnesses".
>
> (Greenblatt, 1991: 56)

From the very beginning the identity of the American natives was negated, their culture ignored, their property and even their lives ceased to belong to them. Initially, this process of annihilation occurred only on a symbolic level, in the rite of taking possession in which "the other exists only as an empty sign, a cypher", but within a short time it also manifested its effects on a practical level, with the destruction of the Arawak culture and people. Symbols are powerful; they define rights, intentions and aims.

Columbus's attitude towards the language of the natives of the Caribbean islands was also indicative. On one hand, he admitted he understood nothing of it; on the other, he was sure that the natives told him he could take anything of theirs he wanted, as he noted in his diary after the brief visit that a young Indian "king" paid to him on board his ship anchored off the island of Tortuga. Greenblatt comments:

> The moments of blankness – 'we could not understand . . .,' 'we do not know . . .,' 'we could not explain . . . ,' – are intertwined strangely with the confident assumption that there was no significant barrier to communication or appropriation: 'We passed through many and dissimilar tongues; Our Lord granted us favor with the people who spoke them for they always understood us, and we them. We questioned them, and received their answers by signs, just as if they spoke our language and we theirs.'
>
> (Greenblatt, 1991: 92)

Like other European explorers travelling in this part of the world in those times, Columbus believed that he understood the language and mind of indigenous populations, from whom he was in fact separated by an immeasurable distance. His inexplicable confidence reflects the difficulty

Europeans had in communicating with others and in acknowledging their cultural "otherness". The development of communication requires common ground between interlocutors, ground to which they can refer in order to explore their reciprocal intentions. There was no common ground between Columbus and the Arawak, but Columbus did not worry too much about that: although he did not understand their language, he just *knew* that native "kings" wished to donate him everything they possessed.

Even when the Europeans did make attempts to communicate, they were hindered by their incapacity to imagine the existence of repertoires of meanings different from those of their own culture. In Trinidad, after having failed to entice the natives to his ship by showing them various objects seductive to a European eye, Columbus tried to attract them by improvising a fiesta: "I caused to be brought up to the castle of the poop a tambourine, that they might play it, and some young men to dance, believing that they would draw near to see the festivity". The natives' response was immediate and surprising: "As soon as they observed the playing and dancing, they all dropped their oars and laid hand on their bows and strung them, and each one of them took up his shield, and they began to shoot arrows" (Greenblatt, 1991: 90–1). A textbook example of a misunderstanding due to different cultural frameworks: dancing, a sign of peace for the Spaniards of those times, was a declaration of war for the Trinidadians.

When one-way communication of this kind fails, there are only two possibilities of action: either to develop communications open to the other – a multi-cultural, wearisome and frustrating task for the Europeans, intent on their dream of conquest; or to give up the idea of communicating, take immediate possession of whatever is up for grabs, and exploit the other ruthlessly, starting from the principle that he has no rights, traditions, or dignity worthy of respect. We know what choice the *conquistadores* made. In these events, choices and precedents solemnly established in 1492, stereotypes were laid down which were to influence all forms of encounter between European and other cultures for centuries to come, until well into modern times.

But can we give the name "encounter" to a situation in which the other was not taken into any account, did not speak, did not exist as a human being with certain recognized rights, as we have just seen in the emblematic ritual of "taking possession"? Would it not be more exact to speak of domination, overwhelming abuse of power, slavery? If the other has no principles, values or valid traditions which defend him, then he is not even a real human being. He is not an adult capable of looking after himself. He must be supervised by those who have higher moral principles, more rational science, a truer religion. It was for these reasons that Columbus proposed to his masters, for "the welfare of the souls of the said cannibals", to send every year from Spain ships full of cattle and other supplies for the colonization of the country, and that payment for these things could be made in slaves, from among these cannibals, a people very savage and suitable for the purpose, and well made and of very good intelligence. We believe that they, having abandoned that inhumanity, will be better than any other slaves, and their inhumanity they will immediately lose when they are out of their own land.

(Greenblatt, 1991: 71)

1492: A CROSSROADS

According to Columbus, the "cannibals" were intelligent but not really human. So, fortunately for them, they could be changed by educational slavery. Queen Isabella, stricken by conscience, did have the sale of the Indians halted immediately and ordered that those who were already in Spain should be confiscated from their owners and sent back to their original islands. But not even the sovereign's supreme power could restrain the appetites of the colonists for long: the slave trade towards the Americas developed all the same but involved black populations from Africa, while the Indians were cruelly treated but not formally enslaved, being now relatively protected by the Spanish royal edicts.

For centuries, the slave trade was one of the greatest sources of profit for both American colonies and European nations. Some of the rich revenue from this traffic went to the owners of the slave fleets, who used part of it to construct the beautiful buildings and churches still adorning the most eminent French and English cities of the Atlantic and the English Channel. Centuries ago, slavery and the black slave trade were not crimes against humanity, as they are today, but good business, blessed by priests and magistrates. Justification for the capture, transport and sale of black people as slaves, or for their being kept in slavery in such sophisticated societies as existed in the southern United States until the first half of the nineteenth century, was not lacking.

Even prestigious and illuminated statesmen like the American president Thomas Jefferson kept slaves and maintained, or at least tolerated, slavery, in spite of negative public opinion in some quarters and the possible prickings of their own conscience. The hateful prejudices of today are often rooted in the iniquitous laws of yesterday. The anachronistic colonial ventures of Italy in Africa during the early twentieth century offered many Italian political and religious authorities the opportunity to state that to force "civilization" on "barbarous" populations who were not interested in it was fully justified. These and similar occurrences compel us to recognize that responsibility for possible present prejudice may often be ascribed to the past behaviour of respected institutions like governments and churches.

What happens to the "other" when their identity is ignored and their home destroyed? Let us consider an episode of the conquest of Mexico by Cortez. In 1524, immediately after the fall of Tenochtitlan, the Franciscan friars invited the few Aztec lords who had survived the massacre to religious colloquies in the conquered city. These took place in the entrance hall of the monastery of St Francis, in a desolate framework of destruction which contrasted violently with the supposedly unchallenged "taking of possession" of 1492. At the end of these talks, one of the Aztec lords (the Spanish chronicler noted that he spoke "courteously") made the following speech:

> You have told us that our gods were not true gods. This word you use is new to us, it disturbs us because our ancestors, those who were here before us and who lived upon the earth, were not accustomed to speaking thus. They gave us their rules of life. They believed in their gods, venerated them and honoured them. They are rich and happy. They give people value and authority.
>
> (Leon-Portilla, 1964: 63)

Deprived of their gods, the Indians no longer possessed either values or authority, not only in the eyes of the Spaniards, but also in their own: "Their ancestral heritage was reduced, in their own words, to 'a net full of holes'". Their world had collapsed: "What had constituted the sense and interpretation of the world became a persecuted, marginalized, discredited rite, a false belief, an error to be rejected and abjured, a sin to be confessed before the ecclesiastic court" (Gruzinski, 1988: 25). The pathways of song of the Indians, by means of which they could move through the world and recognize others and themselves, were obliterated for ever.

The negation of the other leads to their destruction, or urges them to emulate their persecutor, in the vain hope of defending oneself against aggression. Many Indians began to use against their enemies the same contempt of alien traditions which had been used against them. They considered the Spaniards to be "madmen", they believed that the friars were malevolent sorcerers come to destroy humanity, and said that the religion of the Europeans was a fairy-tale which signified absolutely nothing.

The other pathway, which our history has until now rarely followed in encounters with other cultures – to the extent that the few individuals who did really listen to each other were considered with suspicion – starts from that crossroads at which we left Columbus in October 1492. Where he chose one path, ignoring the traditions, language and rights of the other, we must now choose the second path, enhancing the cultures, identities and ways of thinking of the other, who is not just black, Jewish or Indian, but maybe handicapped, old or sick – or simply a person who has been trained in a different profession and uses a peculiar jargon, a language that we do not understand and prefer to ignore.

Chapter 3

Metaphors and analogies

GENERATIVE METAPHORS

Our decisions regarding situations perceived as problematic are influenced by the framework in which we collocate them. If we are not aware of this framing effect, we cannot realize that the perspective we adopt to examine a situation is not the only possible one, nor necessarily the best. The most serious case is that of someone who does not perceive that he or she is seeing things from a particular point of view, but who is sure of seeing things just as they are. This kind of conviction makes negotiation and reciprocal adaptation between people difficult, because it does not admit of plausible alternative ways of viewing things.

The role of metaphors in decision-making depends precisely on their framing function. Metaphors are our permanent house-guests. They are emitted, so linguists assure us, at the rate of four a minute by a standard speaker. "Laura is an angel", "Richard is a skunk", "Barbara is a doll" are everyday examples. A metaphor links someone or something to someone or something existing in another domain of reality. The subject of the sentence is the "target" of the metaphor – in the above examples, "Laura", "Richard", "Barbara" are targets. The element of the sentence which gives us information about the target is the "origin" of the metaphor (in our example "angel", "skunk" and "doll").

If I say "Laura is my sister", I do not produce a true metaphor, because (as long as Laura is indeed my sister in real life) I have not linked two different domains of experience. But I do create a metaphor if the Laura I am talking about is a red hen, or Petrarch's beloved lady, or a hologram of a girl produced by a computer program. The fact that the two domains linked through the metaphor are separate in reality is not always easy to establish, so we may be unable to distinguish the literal meaning from the metaphorical one. In fact, we cannot even be sure that something like a "literal" meaning exists, since any statement we make is caught up in the multi-dimensional, virtually infinite web with which culture provides its members in order to allow them to connect different regions of reality.

We use metaphors to take our bearings in situations and to communicate with others. Metaphors are particularly necessary in situations which, lacking any apparently obvious framework, require solid interpretative guidelines. By means of metaphors, new situations are provided with indications, which may be helpful or otherwise but which are in any case necessary. The metaphors we use in problem-setting have a profound influence on the subsequent problem-solving; Schön (1979) calls them "generative metaphors" because they exert a strong influence on decision-making. He gives as an example of the power of "generative metaphors" the debate on slums in the United States in recent decades. Slums are commonly known as degraded areas of large cities; but there are two different ways of considering them, each based on its own "generative" metaphor.

On one hand, we may consider slums as a "disease" threatening the health of the entire city. Once this metaphor has been chosen, others taken from the field of medicine quickly follow. In order to bring back health to urban communities, we should appeal to experts. And what do the experts say? What do city planners and architects advise? A surgical operation, of course: demolition. The best solution is to move slum residents somewhere else, raze everything to the ground, and rebuild from scratch. The metaphor of disease embodies the idea that slums are an infection or a cancer to be eliminated.

On the other hand, we may choose to see slums not as infected buboes on the healthy body of the city, but as true, vital "communities", whose inhabitants have a story in common and feel a sense of belonging which is unknown in other areas of the city. Slums are thus considered merely as quarters inhabited by low-income people, and the main problem is that there is not much money around. The decision suggested by this different metaphor is that people dwelling in slums should not be removed from them and dispersed, but helped to develop their positive potentials to the full, for example, their special propensity for helping their neighbours.

The first metaphor recommends that slums be demolished and replaced with something else; the second considers slum residents as citizens gifted with appreciable resources but needing financial aid from the city. So instead of town-planners we have social services, which are required to help develop slum communities. These two solutions to the problem arise from different perspectives incorporated in the initial metaphors. Different metaphors tell different stories. There is not a first moment in which we see problems "objectively", as they really are, and a later moment of assessment, influenced by our aims and values, in which we resolve problems and take decisions.

Decisions are initiated at the very moment we pose our problem in a certain way. The two metaphors stimulate different views of what slums are and how their problems should be faced: if they are a cancer, they should be eliminated; if they are vital communities, they should be maintained. Each of the two metaphors offers a different interpretation of an ambiguous situation. Is there an "objective" or "rational" method for establishing which view is the correct one? We believe not, because our judging activity is taken up in the net of presumptions which culture extends over reality.

PROFESSIONS AS CULTURES

A metaphor is not merely a figure of speech. It is essentially a way of perceiving, classifying and evaluating things. If I say to a friend: "My marriage is a prison", I construct a category which contains both my own marriage and prison and, by the same act, I state that these two apparently separate domains have some important characteristics in common. I believe that there are essential features of prison which may also be found in my marriage: this is what the metaphor states and this is the message it conveys to my interlocutor who, naturally enough, may not know which are the characteristics that my marriage shares with prison in my mind and may therefore have trouble in trying to understand what I mean exactly by using this metaphor.

Do I mean that I am really locked up in my room after 10 p.m. or that I miss the wild celebrations which, when we were still bachelors, inevitably followed every victory of our favourite soccer team? My friend will in any case understand that my marriage and prison are, in my mind, linked in a significant way – this is the basic task of a metaphor. It is not an elliptic comparison but an act by means of which I assign objects to categories: I do not say that my marriage is *like* a prison, but that it *is* a prison. There is a clearcut difference between the two: in the first sense, a city planner might think that slums *can be seen as* a kind of disease; in the second sense, he believes that they *are* buboes threatening the health of the city.

Why is it that, faced with the same problem, one person chooses the first metaphor, that of disease, while another chooses the second, that of a vital community? What reasons induce one person to formulate the problem along certain lines and another to formulate the same (or only apparently the same) problem along others? If we recall the way in which the Dyirbal constructed their categories putting women, fireflies, scorpions and stars in the same class, we can answer: experience and culture – in fact, we know that experience and culture are not separate entities but a single one, since people's experiences are moulded by their culture.

For a city planner with an engineering background, a well-known design architect, a super-manager interested in urban mega-projects and mega-contracts, which of the two slum metaphors will appear more appropriate? Probably the first, because it is more obvious "from their point of view". Cynics might say this is also because great planners and managers are sensitive to the prospects of huge earnings as a result of slum demolition and reconstruction. Although such considerations may carry some weight, this is very probably not the only criterion at stake. Much weight must be assigned to people's mentalities, acquired by means of their professional training, which makes them focus their attention on certain things and blinds them to others. The metaphor they choose will be the one which most appeals to the professional interests and competences of the decision-makers.

Modern professions are becoming cultures in themselves. They lead their members to see things in a certain way, to focus on certain aspects of situations, to favour the solutions they can control best. Widely differing conceptions and professions have come into conflict on the question of slums. If the two factions, technological and social, had been able to collaborate with each other, the slum debate would have been more profitable. Instead of maintaining rigid positions on their own metaphors, the decision-makers would have been able to work together, to see which slum areas had decayed beyond recovery and which contained poor but vital communities deserving help. The combined mental resources of city planners, architects, psychologists and social workers would have coalesced to focus on the problem of what to do with inner-city slums.

Why did this not happen? Why does the development of professions occur in a social context which does not worry about creating common ground with others? Some will say that this is the price we must pay for the exponential growth of specialization, which makes encyclopaedic knowledge impossible. Others believe that the situation does not depend only on the great quantity of information which modern societies produce, but also on choices made by the institutions which train the professionals. A quick glance at the study curricula of university faculties shows that these institutions are at present not particularly interested in forming bonds between the various disciplines they teach, and even less interested in trying to open the minds of their students towards interests cultivated by other disciplines in other faculties.

As universities educate students according to a sectorial approach to knowledge, it is not surprising if the resulting graduates are often people who tend to close their competence in a hermetic shell and remain impervious to other perspectives. The problem is not one of legitimate attachment to one's own discipline or profession, but lack of esteem and hostility towards other mentalities. Donald Norman (1992) says that designers' thinking is often so far removed from that of ordinary people that they do not have an exact picture of how the objects they design will be used in daily life by common folk. In spite of this, technical designers do not think they need help from the social scientists, whose knowledge they consider inferior. The postmodern societies in which we live rub shoulders with *classic* prejudices – ethnic, religious, etc. – and with a series of *fresh* prejudices originating from new professions. And these, as we shall see, are just as dangerous as the old ones.

MENTAL LEAPS

Analogies, like metaphors, play an important role in our thought processes. We cannot do without them in our daily reasoning, although they do not supply us with incontrovertible certainties. An analogy is a "mental leap" (Holyoak and Thagard, 1995) from one reality domain to another, by means of which we try to interpret a dubious situation by comparing it with another situation which we have clearly in our minds. Like all similarities, that on which an analogy is based only works from certain viewpoints. An analogy offers illuminating explanations only to the extent in which the similarity it highlights is really pertinent. We cannot know *a priori* whether the similarity we establish between the ambiguous situation before us and the other situation which we use as an analogic explanation of the first will guide us to a satisfactory interpretation and a wise decision.

Analogies permit plausible conjectures, not irrefutable conclusions. The American president Lyndon Johnson compared the political state of affairs in Asia with a game of dominoes and stated that, if Vietnam fell entirely under Communist control, the whole of South-East Asia would follow it. The "domino theory", pronounced as the official doctrine of the American administration during the Vietnam conflict, became an unquestionable dogma; those who doubted it were suspected of disloyalty. History showed that the domino analogy was misleading: mistaking a simple conjecture for absolute truth proved disastrous.

Another example comes from a more recent political and military conflict. American policy and the reactions of public opinion during the 1991 Gulf War, with United Nations and American forces arrayed against Saddam Hussein's Iraq, were based on a series of analogies pivoting around the identification of Saddam with Hitler (Spellman and Holyoak, 1992). The assessment which analogic mapping suggested was evident: it was just and necessary to attack Saddam, as it would have been to declare war on Hitler after the German invasion of Czechoslovakia; if the democratic countries had reacted immmediately on that occasion in 1938, instead of waiting for Poland to be attacked a year later, the world would have been spared much grief.

It is difficult to judge how well-founded this analogy was. Analogic mapping is not a question of truth or falsehood, but of greater or lesser plausibility. It is an attempt to understand an intricate situation by exploiting similarities of the type: invasion of Kuwait = invasion of Czechoslovakia; Iraqi dictatorship = Nazi dictatorship, despite the obviously profound differences between Germany in the 1930s and Iraq in the 1990s. For every aspect of the situation which confirmed analogic mapping, there was another which remained excluded from it: if Saddam was Hitler, who was the American president Bush – Churchill, Roosevelt or Stalin? The map worked with respect to the main villain of the piece, but not for the other characters.

It is not always accepted that ambiguous situations may be seen from various points of views, as a charming little Jewish story illustrates (Atlan, 1987). A wise rabbi was called upon to settle a quarrel between two men. He listened to the first man, reflected on the problem for a while, and then stated that the plaintiff was right. But when the second man told his version of the facts, the rabbi, after another pause for reflection, decided that he too was right. His disciples protested that he could not say that both plaintiffs were right. So the rabbi pondered a little more and concluded: "You too are right". Controversies usually arise over opinable matters in which analogies and metaphors play a role which does not have the compelling logical power of theorems.

ANALOGIES AND PROBLEM-SETTING

Analogies are often used to solve not only political matters but also moral ones. This happens when the problem in question cannot be resolved simply by applying a pre-existing rule but requires imagination (Johnson, 1993). A critical issue to contemporary moral conscience is the rightness or otherwise of abortion. The pros and cons arouse strong feelings not only because there are now many forms of contraception which were previously unknown or because couples now tend to plan their families more carefully than before, but particularly because of the clash between two fundamental principles in modern Western cultures: the sacredness of human life on one hand, and the value of freedom for all human beings, including women, on the other. It is precisely this clash between principles which makes the whole question of abortion particularly dramatic and, for many, confusing. Analogy works as an "intuition pump" (Holyoak and Thagard, 1995) which leads people to see things from one point of view rather than another according to its suggestions, as the following examples provided by the same authors show.

The American moral philosopher Jarvis Thomson proposes this singular scenario. Let us concede, for the sake of the argument, he says, that a fetus is a person. Now let us imagine that a woman wakes up one morning to discover that she has been kidnapped and is lying in a hospital bed, where she lies hooked up by a series of tubes to a famous violinist who is unconscious. The violinist had nothing to do with the kidnapping but he needs to remain attached to the woman for nine months, because his kidneys are not functioning and the woman's blood is compatible with his. After nine months, his kidneys will have recovered sufficiently to allow him to survive on his own, and the woman will be able to do whatever she likes without the unfortunate man's life being in danger.

Is the woman morally obliged to remain attached to the violinist? Although the wretched man is innocent of the kidnapping of the woman and would die if he were disconnected, in Thomson's view the woman was forced into the situation without her knowledge or consent; his example highlights the violence inflicted on the woman by the kidnapping and her compulsory connection to the violinist. The analogy is constructed so that we are led to conclude that the woman does not really have any obligation towards the violinist. No one would criticize her if she made a bid for freedom and abandoned the violinist to his fate.

This analogy contains some characteristics of the situation but ignores others. For example, a fetus certainly cannot be considered as completely extraneous to a woman (geneticists and even socio-biologists, not just moralists, would be horrified at such an enormity); the situation in which a woman finds herself hosting a fetus is not one of severe restriction of freedom; and the origin of a pregnancy is not necessarily the result of a violent act like kidnapping but one of the most precious gifts for a woman and for her community. If we bear these aspects in mind, Thomson's analogic map might appear grotesque. A person considering it as a given fact instead of a somewhat shakily constructed conjecture would show a singular lack of discernment.

Another American moral philosopher, James Huber, suggests a different analogy which primes the "pump of intuition" against the rightness of abortion. Let us imagine, he says, that the victim of a shipwreck has managed to climb on to a floating piece of wreckage and that another survivor, who cannot swim, suddenly appears and asks to be saved. As long as there is space for the newcomer, the first shipwrecked sailor is obliged to allow the newcomer to save themselves, otherwise the first sailor would be guilty of something approaching murder. This analogy highlights the fact that, if the first person refuses to help the second, their action is not justified by a legitimate desire to save their own life, since there is space for both of them. Of course also this analogy has evident deficiencies: the body of the woman is not a floating piece of wreckage to be used as a mere life-raft. The relationship linking a mother to her child is more intimate and demanding than the one existing between the two survivors, and so on.

My aim in stressing the conjectural character of these analogies is to show that they direct our decision-making from the very moment the problem is framed. If we are not aware of the intrinsic limitations of our cognitive processes, we will never be able to understand why other people see things so differently from ourselves. Old and new forms of prejudice are rooted in the arrogance of those who only recognize their own point of view and their own cultural framework.

Part II

Immeasurable distances

"When we leave home and cross our nation's boundaries, moral clarity often blurs. Without a backdrop of shared attitudes, and without familiar laws and judicial procedures that define standards of ethical conduct, certainty is elusive." Is this the complaint of a Moroccan *sans papiers* just arrived in the sinful *ville lumière*, or that of a Mexican peasant who has eluded the border police and now, as an illegal alien, is trying to cope with the puzzling world of the gringos? Neither one nor the other. The words are those of Thomas Donaldson (1996), of the University of Pennsylvania, as they appeared in the *Harvard Business Review*. He expresses the unease of American companies working abroad, whose personnel often have to deal with mentalities very far from those to which they are accustomed.

There is the famous case of a computer company which obliged its managers in Saudi Arabia to follow a course on sexual harassment. Those taking the course were asked to discuss situations like that of a manager making obvious advances to the new secretary while they have a drink together. The course designers did not realize that the situation was offensive for pious Muslims, and ridiculous in a country where men and women are strictly segregated and alcohol is officially banned for religious reasons. Donaldson blames the *faux pas* on "ethic imperialism": the idea that there is only one moral world which need be considered – one's own. At times like the present, when even distant areas of the planet form part of a single global village, it is essential to be aware of the depth of cultural differences.

Chapter 4, *Different shipwrecks*, illustrates two basically opposite attitudes towards differences. The Spanish *conquistador* Alvar Nuñez, shipwrecked naked off the coast of Florida, abandoned his previous habits and customs and lived for seven years as a shaman among the local Indians, having acquired a new, transcultural identity, both of Spanish *and* Indian. Conversely, Defoe's hero Robinson Crusoe, shipwrecked with all his clothes on, succeeded in dominating his exotic island with the tools of his original culture: he became rich, but did not change or enrich his identity.

Chapter 5, *Hopes of happiness*, shows what bottomless abysses may sometimes yawn between cultures. Gestures like *suttee*, honoured by Hindu tradition, cause us in the West to remain suspended in amazement, horror and fascination. The confusion we feel when faced with radical differences between discrepant value systems shows us just how remote from others we may be. Differences are not insurmountable gaps hindering all sort of communications among different worlds but call for awareness of the fact that gaps can exist and stimulate commitment in building bridges over cultural barriers.

Chapter 6, *So near and yet so far*, considers the conflict which arises between different cultures when they are too close to ignore each other and too distant to find any acceptable agreement among themselves. In Palestine/ Israel, two peoples contend the same territory, the same places of prayer, the same patriarchs. Well-educated young people, model students following prayers assiduously in the temple, do appalling things to "the other side" in the conviction that they are merely fulfilling their duty towards a tradition which they feel is threatened. If we are going to manage to live on the globe together how can we avoid that cultural differences generate or enhance conflicts? On which grounds can we come to acknowledge other mentalities, other faiths, others' claims to our heritage?

Chapter 4

Different shipwrecks

AS NAKED AS BABES

The cultural perspective does away with the currently accepted idea that the individual is the starting point for social interactions. It maintains that it is culture which shapes the identity of individuals, groups and organizations. Just exactly what culture is, is still an open question. In the 1980s the conception of cognitive anthropology developed, according to which culture functions like a computer program.

> Culture is best seen not as complexes of concrete behavior patterns (customs, usages, traditions, habit clusters) but as a set of control mechanisms (plans, recipes, rules, instructions for governing behavior). The "control mechanism" view of culture begins with the assumption that human thought is basically both social and public and that its natural habitat is the house yard, the marketplace, and the town square.
>
> (Geertz, 1973: 44)

This vision, however, is not completely satisfactory because it considers culture as a kind of mould which renders everyone's beliefs and behaviours uniform. This would apply in a world of clones but not in that admirably variegated world in which we live. Nor is it appropriate to speak of "culture" in the singular, as if every society lived in splendid isolation, separated from its neighbours. Every culture has always exchanged ideas, objects and people with others, and still does so. Even countries which decide to avoid all contacts with foreigners, as Japan did in the eighteenth century, and the Soviet Union too after the Second World War, are not impermeable, but stare fixedly at the very worlds they fear and at the same time desire to meet.

Hybridization, encounters and exchanges are the rule and not the exception in the life of cultures. Travel represents the most frequent and popular opportunity for such encounters, even though the development of mass media and mass tourism have considerably reduced the impact of encounters with other cultures, which only 50 years ago was dramatically evident. Today's jet flights promise no real drama because in fact there are no real encounters. When tourists visit faraway countries, sealed in their luxury air-conditioned coaches and hotel rooms, sometimes they do not even bother to look around, occupied as they are in composing that *collage* of ephemeral images (Kearney, 1995) they wish to show their friends back home one Saturday evening.

One can travel towards new worlds, or be shipwrecked on them, with very different outcomes. One may be mentally changed by the experience or simply become wealthy. One may conquer or be conquered. The journey of Alvar Nuñez Cabeza de Vaca began with a proud declaration of intended conquest (1542): "There departed on the fifteenth day of June 1527, from the port of San Lucar de Barrameda, the governor Panfilo de Narvaez, with power and mandate from Your Majesty to conquer and govern the provinces of Tierra Firma between Rio de las Palmas and the Cape of Florida." With these words Alvar Nuñez, treasurer and official supervisor of the fleet, opened his report on the expedition for his sovereign, the emperor Carlos V, written ten years after his departure from Spain. It tells of a terrible disaster and an exalting adventure.

The disaster struck the men of the great expedition, 600 of them, in five ships. At their first landfall on Santo Domingo, 150 soldiers deserted, obliging the whole convoy to waste time in Cuba to replace men and horses. The enterprise was dogged by misfortune: both hurricanes and quarrels blew up violently. Having reached the coast of Florida, the Spaniards, led by their commander-in-chief, disembarked to investigate the territory, lost contact with their ships, and found themselves wandering, hopelessly lost, in an unknown and lethal environment. Clashes with Indian tribes, sickness and starvation all combined against them, so that by the early winter of 1528, of the brave company which had set sail just over a year before from Spain, only four survivors remained, one of whom was Alvar Nuñez.

The adventure, for Alvar Nuñez and his three companions, began at this point, when the protective shell of the institution which had held them broke apart, like the fragile hulls of their ships, leaving them as exposed and vulnerable as newborn babes. Their ships, weapons, clothes, even the little toy bells they had brought from distant Europe to bewitch the natives had disappeared, engulfed in the swamps or lost in the hurricanes. Their makeshift boats, hastily put together in an attempt to escape, were overwhelmed by the fury of the waves. "We were naked as the day we came into the world, deprived of those few things which, in those circumstances, meant everything to us. It was November and the cold was intense. We were reduced to skin and bone, we looked like the image of death" (Cabeza de Vaca, 1542 [1989]: 44).

When the army vanished and, with it, all hopes of conquest, the survivors began a journey which was to take them to the heart of the world they had dreamed of dominating. Those who had thought of enslaving the Indians were captured by those same Indians. Those who had hoped to conquer were themselves conquered in a way which, Alvar Nuñez sensed, it would not be prudent to reveal to his former companions at the end of his wanderings. Seven years later, after infinite and wearisome leagues of travel, when he again found himself in Spanish hands, this time on the Pacific coast, Nuñez called his compatriots "them", "the Christians", and denounced their cruelty towards "us", the native Indians.

Nakedness had marked the beginning of Alvar Nuñez's new life and was to accompany him throughout his wanderings with the Indians. "For this entire period we lived naked and, not being accustomed to this state, we changed our skins twice a year like snakes. Our bodies were covered with sores as a result of exposure to the sun and wind, which caused us great suffering" (Cabeza de Vaca, 1542 [1989]: 78). This state of affairs must have been appalling for a man who, later governor of the province of Rio de la Plata and arrested by a group of Spanish rebels to be shipped back to Spain, jealously guarded in his personal chest, among the few poor possessions still remaining to him (half a candle, and a needle for repairing sails) a splendid gala uniform. When his adventures finally came to an end, for several days Nuñez was not able to bear the contact of clothes on his skin.

CHANGING SKIN

Alvar Nuñez also changed his skin in a deeper sense, as he cautiously informs us in his report. He had become a shaman among the natives: "Throughout that period, many Indios came to seek us out, convinced that we were truly children of the sun." He was immensely proud of his powers as a healer, which he attributed to courage, a virtue he had inherited from his warrior family: "Of the three, I was the most famous for my courage in venturing on any type of treatment. However, there was never anyone who was treated by us and who then said that he was not better. Such was their confidence in us that they were convinced that, as long as we remained with them, no-one would die" (Cabeza de Vaca, 1542 [1989]: 76).

For a Christian, and a Spanish *conquistador*, it was not easy to be, and declare oneself to be, a shaman. For Nuñez, it was not only a question of healing people, finding himself in states of ecstasy, and being able to undertake journeys in which his spirit, separated from his body, flew through the heavens exploring the ways of the cosmos. It was also a vision of divine and human things which was very far from Christian doctrine. Nuñez prudently minimized the importance of his new knowledge. He mentions relatively innocuous practices such as breathing and blowing on his patients, making small cuts on their skin, and placing his hands on them. He states that he always accompanied these acts with Christian blessings and recitals of the Pater Noster and Ave Maria. But he is reticent about the visions and rites which aided him to understand and interpret the religious world of the Indios to the extent that he became their spiritual guide.

Although he played down the shamanistic aspects of his experience as a healer, Nuñez did feel the need to supply a series of justifications for what had happened to him. First of all, he states that he was forced into this position: "They ordered us to act. We laughed, thinking it was a joke, and answered that we were not capable of such things. But they threatened to give us no food until we obeyed. We were forced to do as they said, without fearing that we might be blamed later on for what we did" (Cabeza de Vaca, 1542 [1989]: 52). His reluctance to accept his new role as a healer, probably mentioned in order to avoid possible future accusation of heterodoxy, was typical of the shamanistic tradition, according to which the chosen person initially resisted the call until his vocation was confirmed and almost imposed upon him by persons in authority who then took on the task of completing his religious training.

The vocation to be a shaman was individual but its function social, and as such it required public recognition and formal training. Thus Alvar Nuñez, a Spaniard, a Christian and a *conquistador*, was turned into an Indio shaman. His tale also contains a veiled mention of his native master:

> Faced with our obstinacy, one Indio told me that I was foolish to refuse to profit by his medical knowledge, because the stones and the herbs which grew in the fields possessed great power. He told me that, simply by placing a hot stone on a patient's stomach, he could remove pain. Surely we, who were men, possessed even greater powers than stones and herbs.
>
> (Cabeza de Vaca, 1542 [1989]: 52)

A second justification, which reveals that Nuñez clearly knew he was walking on very thin ice, is found in the passages in which he declares that he is not sure whether his healing treatments had really been effective. They might have been the result of the Indios' credulity, he says, although he was not satisfied with this explanation, which was intended to provide a line of defence against possible future accusations of witchcraft by making little of the magnificence of his extraordinary adventure. The story he was so proud of telling his king and emperor was not that of a charlatan, but of an enlightened man who had accomplished great things in a new and amazing world.

His enthusiasm even led him, on one occasion, to claim a miraculous cure, a resurrection:

> As soon as I reached the village, I realized that the sick man was already dead, both by the number of people weeping around him and by the fact that his home had been dismantled as a sign of mourning. The man's eyes were upturned in his head, he had no pulse, and showed all the

other signs of death. At least, so it seemed to myself and Dorantes. I raised the mat which covered him and with all my faith begged God to grant health to him and to all those who needed it. After I had blessed him and blown on his body many times, the Indios offered me his bow and a basket of figs. Late that night, they came back, saying that the dead man whom I had treated in their presence had got up and walked, eaten, and spoken to them.

(Cabeza de Vaca, 1542 [1989]: 75)

Nuñez's third line of defence consisted of giving an at least generally Christian tone to his activities as a shaman. He carefully records that he prayed to God and blessed his patients before breathing on them and using his powers as a medicine man. He even presents as an exaltation of the Holy Faith his success among the Indians, who followed him in their thousands with awe, passing him from one tribe to another across the country from the Atlantic to the Pacific. "Throughout the territory", he writes, "they could speak of nothing but the marvels which our Lord God had accomplished through us, and so the surrounding tribes came to seek us out, asking us to cure them of their afflictions" (Cabeza de Vaca, 1542: 75). Nuñez even insinuates that it was the design of Providence that he should become a shaman, so that in due course he could be restored to the Spanish, thanks to the freedom he enjoyed as a medicine man and a leader among the natives.

We do not know exactly what Alvar Nuñez had become by the time he recorded his story. Certainly, he was no longer a Christian and a Spaniard as before, but neither was he truly an Indian shaman. He was both something more and something less, and could not be classified in one of the usual categories built on pre-established and socially recognized dichotomies such as Spaniard–Indian, Christian–pagan, and so on. He had become something new, a kind of graft or hybrid, as he himself must have perceived. Now he inhabited the interface between two cultures; he no longer belonged completely to either. He was an interpreter, a bearer of messages ferrying between the two banks of the river which he had crossed at such cost. We know enough to realize that his adventure was unlike that of any other *conquistador* of the time.

Nuñez was transformed by his experience of walking naked among the Indians and, at great personal risk, he tried to tell others what had happened to him so that they too could become aware of his visions (which perhaps he still had) and of the extraordinary powers which had been granted to him. The *conquistador* had been conquered. He changed, became more complete and probably also more uncertain about his identity as a Spaniard and a Christian: at the end of his long journey, he spoke of "we" when referring to himself in the company of the Indians and "they" when referring to his compatriots – he who had been born in Spain and was about to return among his comrades. It is difficult for us now to imagine what this "we" meant for a sixteenth-century Spanish nobleman, for the proud young warrior who had sailed from San Lucar de Barrameda to seek glory and fortune in the New World.

REASON AND DEVOTION

Similar, although opposite in direction and outcome, is the tale of Robinson Crusoe, "Who lived Eight and Twenty Years, all alone in an un-inhabited Island on the Coast of America, near the Mouth of the Great River Oroonoque; Having been cast on Shore by Shipwreck, wherein all the Men perished but himself" (Defoe, 1719 [1972]: 23). Although Robinson Crusoe is an invented character, his figure embodies an articulated rational "model" of moral and profitable conduct; Rousseau considered Defoe's work as one of the happiest treatises on natural education.

The exotic enterprise of Robinson Crusoe, born at York in 1632, offers an idealized reconstruction of the path that an English Puritan of the times was obliged to follow in order to become rich in the New World and at the same time be at peace with his conscience. At the end of his vicissitudes, Crusoe gained immense wealth from his overseas possessions. While Alvar Nuñez found himself, at the end of his journeyings, economically poor but spiritually enriched by his encounter with the Indians, Robinson Crusoe remained the same throughout his entire adventure and was rewarded for his coherence with a pile of pieces-of-eight large enough to satisfy the greediest buccaneer. He became rich but did not experience anything like the powers and awe and bewilderment of the Indian–Spanish shaman Alvar Nuñez.

How could Crusoe change in his encounter with another culture when Defoe, his creator, caused him to be shipwrecked on a desert island, not even as naked as a babe-in-arms but always decently fully clothed? Even later, when the island ceased to be completely deserted the situation did not improve. As soon as the first "other" appeared, Crusoe immediately and obviously assigned to him the role of servant, whom he benevolently cared for, fed, clothed and educated. While Nuñez was initiated by the Indians into their knowledge, nothing of the kind could happen to Crusoe. It was simply unthinkable for Defoe and his readers that the poor good savage Friday would be able (or dare to presume) to teach something to his European master, from whom he had received everything, including his very name.

The island was later populated with innumerable and undesirable "others": first a bunch of savage cannibals disembarked on the other side of the island to celebrate their repulsive rites, and then a mutinous crew of criminal sailors tried to invade Robinson's peaceful domain. Crusoe, a courageous man, was obliged to fight and defeat them with the aid of his guns and of Friday, in the role of henchman, thus restoring his dominion over the island. Here again, his experience differs from that of Nuñez, whose cannibals were not Indians but Spaniards, crazed by deprivation, who had lost their way and their minds in the swamps.

There is definitely something wrong in Crusoe's attitude towards others. His agitation when he discovers he is not alone on the island approaches the comic:

> It happened one day about noon going towards my boat, I was exceedingly surprised with the print of a man's naked foot on the shore, which was very plain to be seen in the sand. I stood like one thunder-struck, or as if I had seen an apparition; I listened, I looked round me, I could hear nothing, nor see any thing; I went up to a rising ground to look farther; I went up the shore and down the shore, but it was all one, I could see no other impression but that one. I went to it again to see if there were any more, and to observe if it might not be my fancy; but there was no room for that, for there was exactly the very print of the foot, toes, heel, and every part of a foot; how it came thither I knew not, nor could in the least imagine. But after innumerable fluttering thoughts, like a man perfectly confused and out of my self, I came home to my fortification, not feeling, as we say, the ground I went on, but terrify'd to the last degree.
>
> (Defoe, 1719 [1972]: 162)

Crusoe's attitude towards "others" is certainly not one of confidence. He behaves like one surrounded by a hostile environment to be kept at bay by force. His exploration of the island begins as follows:

> I found also that the island I was in was barren and, as I saw good reason to believe, un-inhabited, except by wild beasts, of whom however I saw none, yet I saw abundance of fowls, but knew not their kinds, neither when I killed them could I tell what was fit for food, and what not; at my coming back, I shot at a great bird which I saw sitting upon a tree on the side of a great wood. I believe it was the first gun that had been fired there since the creation of the world. As for the creature I killed, I took it to be a kind of a hawk, its colour and beak resembling it, but it had no talons or claws more than common; its flesh was carrion, and fit for nothing.
>
> (Defoe, 1719 [1972]: 71–2)

This useless killing is emblematic of the violent relationship with nature which the Europeans brought with them to the New World.

Crusoe does not encounter another culture, but exploits to the full the resources of his original one. He reasons, makes plans and calculates, like the clever businessman he is. Before starting a task, he prepares an estimate of the situation as a bookkeeper would do with a ledger, with "Evil" written at the top of the left-hand page and "Good" at the top of the right-hand one, on a sheet of paper folded lengthways. His tale may be read as a manual of the ways in which a culture is incorporated in its members and re-created by each of them, provided that they have the necessary artifacts and sufficient courage. This was one reason for the fascination which Defoe's romance had for the readers of his time.

As well as abundant reserves of food, Crusoe manages to save a chest of carpenter's tools, two guns and three Bibles from his sinking ship. With these, he constructs a way of telling the time, a house, fire and bread. He makes pots, mends his clothes, and fashions a parasol to protect him from the burning sun. In actual fact, he does not invent anything at all, but makes what his artifacts allow him to make, or rather suggest that he make. They are embodied projects and, by their very presence and appropriate uses, tell him what things can or must be done and what not, and how (Mantovani, 1996b).

The most important object which Crusoe manages to recover is his Bible, to which he resorts when his self-control wavers:

> The anguish of my soul at my condition would break out upon me on a sudden, and my very heart would die within me, to think of the woods, the mountains, the deserts I was in; and how I was a prisoner, locked up with the eternal bars and bolts of the ocean, in an un-inhabited wilderness, without redemption. In the midst of the greatest composures of my mind, this would break out upon me like a storm, and make me wring my hands and weep like a child. Sometimes it would take me in the middle of my work, and I would immediately sit down and sigh, and look upon the ground for an hour or two together; and this was still worse to me; for if I could burst out into tears, or vent my self by words, it would go off, and the grief exhausted itself would abate. But now I began to exercise my self with new thoughts; I daily read the word of God, and apply'd all the comforts of it to my present state.
>
> (Defoe, 1719 [1972]: 125)

Crusoe is self-administering his own Sunday sermon. He does really discover a culture, to which he clings, but it is the same culture he had before. Now, in his remote island, he is an even more pious Puritan than he had been in England. Thanks to the combined forces of reason and devotion, he remains the same throughout his trials. The same cannot be said of Alvar Nuñez, who in the end was so confused about his own identity that he said "we" of himself and the Indians and "they" of his old Spanish comrades. Robinson Crusoe remained faithful to himself and became rich: a model for his countrymen. Nuñez changed his skin: he had to remove from himself the suspicion of being a traitor.

THE TWO FACES OF TRAVEL

In the end, both Alvar Nuñez and Robinson Crusoe returned to their homes, although their booty in each case was different. Alvar Nuñez the Spaniard extended his identity to embrace the world of the Indians, although it probably cost him dear. Robinson Crusoe the Englishman proved his endurance and initiative in a hostile environment and accumulated a fortune. Of the two, Alvar Nuñez probably gained the prize that many of us covet. At the end of his travels, his identity could no longer be defined in binary terms – *either* Spanish *or* Indian; it is easier to understand using additive terms – *both* Spanish *and* Indian. In this sense, Alvar Nuñez is an extremely modern figure: he shares parts of his identity with one community and other parts of it with another. Anthropologists, referring to the growing number of people who incessantly migrate from one country to another, have noticed the massive emergence of transcultural identities which do not fall into official categories because they arise in those unofficial spaces which are transnational communities, informal economies, boundary areas populated by persons "*sans papiers*" (Kearney, 1995).

When a journey leads us to expand the boundaries of our identity to the point at which we include in the "we" what was previously simply "other", our journey is a return home, we come full circle. At a certain moment in 1954, in the corner of a square in Marrakesh where he had never been before, Elias Canetti, Nobel prize-winner for literature in 1981, a Bulgarian Jew who had originally lived in Vienna, and fled from the Nazis to London and then Zurich, felt that he had finally returned home. "I seemed to have reached the goal of my journeyings. I no longer wished to leave that place, I had been there hundreds of years before but had forgotten it, and suddenly it all came back to me. While I stood here, I *was* that square. I believe I had always been that square. It was so painful for me to leave it that I kept coming back to it every five or ten minutes" (Canetti, 1964: 57).

But the bright face of travel, which consists of the experience of finding in faraway lands an unknown piece of oneself, as happened in different ways for Nuñez and Canetti, also possesses its dark side. In encounters with other worlds, the desire to overpower the other may prevail, especially if that other is unable to defend himself. Canetti's story reveals a trace of this. A short distance from the magic square, while eating supper with friends, he recognizes some children he knows. They cluster round the open door of the restaurant and begin to make jokes pretending to wear the whiskery moustaches which Canetti and his friends wear.

A little girl of about ten, the prettiest of the group, pretends that she has a moustache too, preens her little whiskers, and laughs happily with her playfellows. Canetti writes:

The restauranteur came to our table to receive our orders and saw the laughing children. With a radiant expression, he said: "That one there already behaves like a little whore". I was disturbed by such an insinuation and asked innocently, "What are you saying? Surely not at that age". "Don't you know", the man replied, "that for fifty francs you could have any of those children? For such a sum any of them would jump at the chance of coming round the corner with you".

(Canetti, 1964: 104)

When meeting dissimilar cultures, occasions for reciprocal growth open, but so do spaces for ever new forms of violence, enhanced by the unbalance of power which exists in various areas of the world. Tourism for sex, which Canetti perceived in his beloved square, now involves many children in ways which mainly escape control and punishment by local authorities and also in their native Western countries. The result is a true assault on the children of the poorest societies on earth, as reported but still unfortunately not halted, by various international aid organizations. Our contacts with different worlds may open the way to abuse unless they are accompanied by the utmost respect.

Travel, today as in the times of the *conquistadores*, places people in the position of having to make a choice: do they want to dominate the other, or do they wish to listen to the other? A journey is a space in which not only distant countries but also the identity of the traveller is discovered:

"The self is at stake in moments of choice and deliberation. Human beings are not fixed quasi-objects that have an independent prior identity and *then* go about making choices from which they are distanced. We are, rather, beings in process whose identity emerges and is continually transformed in an ongoing process of reflection and action. Our actions express who we are, and they may also transform who we are at the same time" (Johnson, 1993: 12).

In encounters with other cultures we both reveal and construct ourselves. When crossing the boundaries between different worlds we are confronted by a moral dilemma: is our aim conquest or exploration, domination or meeting with other people on the basis of equals rights?

Communication among different cultural worlds is inscribed in and supported by pre-existing social relationships, contrary to our view of communication as a purely individual process. While "communication among strangers is definitely not the norm in collectivist cultures" (Greenfield, 1997), we in the West assume that communication can flow freely among parties which are not previously linked in significant and socially recognized ways. Cultural context makes possible communication, not *vice versa*.

Chapter 5

Hopes of happiness

FABULOUS MONSTERS

Although encounters with other cultures may allow us to extend the confines of our personal and social identity, they may also be profoundly confusing. Sometimes a little humour is sufficient to bridge the gap, as in the case of the meeting between Alice and the Unicorn:

> When his eye happened to fall upon Alice [the Unicorn] turned round instantly, and stood for some time looking at her with an air of the deepest disgust. "What – is – this?" he said at last. "This is a child!" Haigha replied eagerly, coming in front of Alice to introduce her, and spreading out both his hands towards her in an Anglo-Saxon attitude. "We only found it to-day. It's as large as life, and twice as natural!" "I always thought they were fabulous monsters!" said the Unicorn. "It is alive?" "It can talk," said Haigha, solemnly. The Unicorn looked dreamily at Alice, and said "Talk, child." Alice could not help her lips curling up into a smile as she began: "Do you know, I always thought Unicorns were fabulous monsters, too! I never saw one alive before!" "Well, now that we *have* seen each other," said the Unicorn, "if you'll believe in me, I'll believe in you. Is that a bargain?" "Yes, if you like," said Alice.
>
> (Carroll, 1872 [1984]: 119–20)

The Unicorn views Alice as a monster because he has never seen anything like her before. Once his initial surprise is over, he easily recognizes her, provided that the recognition is mutual. Alice accepts this, and the meeting between two fabulous monsters ends in mutual understanding.

However, things are not so simple when we come up against something which we consider monstrous because it appears morally repugnant to us. If we choose to ignore this sort of situation, we deny or conceal the real depth of cultural differences. In fact, cultures may be so different that what shines as a splendid gesture in the eyes of the members of one culture may seem horrible to the members of another. The traditional practice of *suttee* in the Hindu world was believed to be eradicated as a result of the tenacious efforts of the British administrators during their long dominion over India. But it is not, as shown by a relatively recent episode which made headlines in the Indian press and on television.

On 4 September 1987, an 18-year-old Rajput girl, Roop Kanwar, a university student, immolated herself on the funeral pyre of her dead husband, cradling his head on her lap. *Suttee* took place before a crowd chanting prayers, and a votive chapel was erected on the spot. Richard Shweder (1991), professor of cultural anthropology at the University of Chicago, reports that Indian public opinion was divided on the matter. Opposers of *suttee* believed that the girl had been forced to kill herself, was drugged or out of her mind with grief, and that her action was execrable. Supporters saw her as a heroine, a saint, almost a goddess, her action to be hailed as a noble gesture. Between opposers and supporters there was no space for tacit agreement, as between Alice and the Unicorn. The contrast could not have been greater.

For us in the West, our position in such a dispute is clearly laid down for us right from the start by our culture, which does not contemplate anything similar to *suttee*, an action rooted in the deepest values of Hinduism.

> Suttee works, for those for whom it works, as a representation and confirmation through heroic action of some of the deepest properties of Hinduism's moral world. In that world existence is imbued with divinity. . . . Hindu moral doctrine has it that husbands and wives live in the world as gods and goddesses. She is the Laxmi of the house; he is her Narayan. As gods and goddesses their bonds to each other are transcendental and eternal. Yet they are incarnate. They are able to dance and eat and make love and transgress and sin; there is a place for the demonic in a romantic world. And they are able to die, which means that from time to time they must shed their vulnerable human form and be newly born again, male and female, as a lizard, as an owl, as a dog, as a human being.
>
> (Shweder, 1991: 16)

For Hindus, death is not a definitive exit from this world, as it is for Christians, but a threshold which is crossed many times. The true problem, for a Hindu, is *how* this threshold should be crossed.

> In the Hindu moral world the death of a husband has more than material significance, and its metaphysical meanings run deep. Traditional widows in India spend the balance of their lives absolving themselves of sin (fasting, praying, withdrawing from the world, reading holy texts). In their world of retributive causation, widowhood is a punish-

ment for past transgressions. The fact that your husband died first is a sign telling you that you must now undertake the task of unburdening yourself of guilt, for the sake of your next incarnation on earth. A shared cremation absolves sins and guarantees eternal union between husband and wife, linked to each other as god and goddess through the cycle of future rebirths.

(Shweder, 1991: 16)

Suttee does not only accumulate good *kharma* for future reincarnations but also offers a noble alternative to the life of penitence and mortification which awaits a Hindu widow. For her it is not an act of self-punishment, as it inevitably is for those who do not share the Hindu vision of the world. It is possible that Roop Kanwar acted like a devout Hindu. The fact that we cannot *understand* her gesture in terms of our own culture, which is the only map we have to guide us, does not mean that her conduct was meaningless. We are dealing with cultural difference, not with folly. "The inconsistency between Roop Kanwar's view of suttee and Allan Blooms's (or a feminist's, for that matter) is not something we need to resolve; it is something we need to seek, so that through astonishment we may stay on the move between different worlds, and in that way become more complete" (Shweder, 1991: 19). If distances are immense, at least we know that they are so and can prepare ourselves for the possibility that, every now and then, we may be called upon to wonder at their immensity.

AMAZEMENT, FASCINATION AND HORROR

Europeans were torn between fascination and horror at the spectacle of *suttee*. It is easy to speak in theoretical terms of cultural differences but a very different matter to decide what to do when those same differences present themselves in flesh and blood and oblige us to take up a position. Geertz (1983), an anthropologist at the University of Princeton, quotes the case of a British officer in nineteenth-century India who was so convinced by the argument of a Hindu widow that, apparently, he allowed her to celebrate *suttee*. But basically Westerners were unable to view it as other than a barbarous, inhuman rite, although they recognized its heroic and even sacred character. Disgust was always mixed with fascination, as revealed by the tale of an eye-witness, Helms, a Dane serving a white rajah in southern Bali between 1839 and 1856. He was present at a *suttee* ceremony on 20 December 1847, after the death of the rajah of a nearby state (1882, quoted in Geertz, 1983).

The narrative opens with a joyful scene: *suttee* is a festival and fifty thousand people had come from all parts of the island to take part in it.

It was a lovely day, and along the soft and slippery paths by the embankments which divide the lawn-like terraces of an endless succession of paddy-fields, groups of Balinese in festive attire, could be seen wending their way to the place of burning. Their gay dresses stood out in bright relief against the tender green of the ground over which they passed. The whole surroundings bore an impress of plenty, peace, and happiness, and, in a measure, of civilization.

(Helm in Geertz, 1983: 37)

Helms felt this festive atmosphere was quite out of place: "It was hard to believe that within a few miles of such a scene, three women, guiltless of any crime, were, for their affection's sake, and in the name of religion, to suffer the most horrible of deaths, while thousands of their countryman looked on" (Helm in Geertz, 1983: 37) He carefully describes the slowly advancing funeral procession. The great decorated tower of wood on which the body of the rajah was laid was followed by three smaller towers, decorated less lavishly, on which the three young concubines stood. Helms was bewildered: a man who had been brought up on stories of knights who saved maidens from the jaws of fiery dragons was about to witness the spectacle of three "guiltless" girls burnt to death before an ecstatic crowd!

The women's composure was admirable:

The victims of this cruel superstition showed no signs of fear at the terrible doom now so near. Dressed in white, their long black hair partly concealing them, with a mirror in one hand and a comb in the other, they appeared intent only upon adorning themselves as though for some gay festival. The courage which sustained them in a position so awful was extraordinary, but it was born of the hope of happiness in a future world. From being bondswomen here, they believed they were to become the favourite wives and queens of their late master in another world. They were assured that their readiness to follow him to a future world, with cheerfulness and amid pomp and splendour, would please the unseen powers, and induce the great god Shiva to admit them without delay to the Swerga Surya, the heaven of Indra.

(Helm in Geertz, 1983: 38)

As the rite approached its culmination, Helms was increasingly impressed by the girls' serenity:

The women were carried in procession three times round the place [of cremation] and then lifted on to the fatal bridge. There they waited until the flames had consumed the image [a wooden simulacre of a lion containing the body of the dead raja]. Still they showed no fear, still their chief care seemed to be the adornment of the body, as though making ready for life rather than for death. The rail at the further end of the bridge was opened, and a plank was pushed over the flames, and attendants below poured quantities of oil on the fire, causing bright, lurid flames to shoot up to a great height. The supreme moment had arrived.

(Helm in Geertz, 1983: 39)

A flight of doves then appeared to express the meaning of the ceremony:

With firm and measured steps the victims trod the fatal plank; three times they brought their hands together over their heads, on each of which a small dove was placed, and then, with body erect, they leaped into the flaming sea below, while the doves flew up, symbolizing the escaping spirits. Two of the woman showed, even at the very last, no sign of fear; they looked at each other, to see whether both were prepared, and then, without stopping, took the plunge. The third appeared to hesitate, and to take the leap with less resolution; she faltered for a moment, and then followed, all three disappearing without uttering a sound.

(Helm in Geertz, 1983: 39)

Helms was too acute and too honest a witness not to perceive and describe to us that the women seemed to be going towards life and not death. Yet what his Western eyes registered was a scene of death, because that is how he categorized what was happening. He believed that the women were wrong, deluded by false beliefs, and that beyond the flames there was no world of happiness with their lord, but only black fate. Why did he consider as unfounded the hope of happiness in a future world which sustained the rajah's intrepid concubines in their leap to death? Why should his vision of things be worth more than the Hindu vision, which after all boasts an illustrious tradition?

ENCOUNTERS AND UNCERTAINTIES

In late Medieval times, this kind of question was given a very simple answer, that found in the *Chanson de Roland*: "*payens ont tort et chrétiens ont droit*". Eighteenth-century Europeans were equally certain of their right to dominate far-off lands, but they believed that this right was based on the moral, scientific and technological superiority of their civilization with respect to that of other cultures – in spite of the "plenty, peace, and happiness" which Helms noted in the solemn scene on Bali which he described for us. His tale concludes thus:

It was a sight never to be forgotten by those who witnessed it, and brought to one's heart a strange feeling of thankfulness that one belonged to a civilization which, with all its faults, is merciful, and tends more and more to emancipate women from deception and cruelty. To the British rule it is due that this foul plague of *suttee* is extirpated in India, and doubtless the Dutch have, ere now, done as much for Bali. Works like these are the credentials by which the Western civilization makes good its right to conquer and humanize barbarous races and to replace ancient civilizations.

(Helm in Geertz, 1983: 39)

The bewildering spectacle of *suttee* led Helms to state that Western values were the only ones with true moral dignity and that the colonial authorities who required them to be respected were justified in their attempt to "replace ancient civilizations". European statesmen, merchants, missionaries and scientists believed for centuries that human progress followed a single linear path and that all cultures had their place in it, at some point along a continuum which, starting from the most backward forms, gradually rose step by step to achieve culture *par excellence* – modern Western culture. This concept is now rejected both by cultural anthropology (Shweder, 1991) and cultural psychology (Cole, 1996; Wertsch et al., 1995) which have both fully recognized the qualitative – and not just quantitative – diversity of human cultures, claimed as long ago as 1920 by Frank Boas.

The assumption that our world of values is better, more just and rational than that of others, rests on fragile foundations. Europeans did not practise *suttee*, but they devoted themselves wholeheartedly to hunting down witches, burning heretics, trafficking in African slaves and exterminating the Indians of the New World. The list of grievances which may be presented to Western civilization is long and its most recently added items are spine-chilling: two world wars, the Holocaust, the dropping of two atom bombs, widespread contamination of the environment, and the destruction of natural equilibria throughout the planet. If we abandon the reassuring conviction that our way of seeing things is the best, we find ourselves in a world which reserves many surprises for us, not all of them pleasant.

We become more uncertain, more confused, more perplexed, as Geertz (1983) wisely remarks:

Whatever use the imaginative production of other peoples – predecessors, ancestors, or distant cousins – can have for our moral lives, then, it cannot be to simplify them. The image of the past (or the primitive, or the classic, or the exotic) as a source of remedial wisdom, a prosthetic corrective for a damaged spiritual life – an image that has governed a good deal of humanist thought and education – is mischievous because it leads us to expect that our uncertainties will be reduced by access to thought-worlds constructed along lines alternative to our own, when in fact they will be multiplied.

(Geertz, 1983: 44–5)

Ours is a merciful civilization, said Helms, meaning by this mercy towards women. This may be partly true: in the Western world, women have recently acquired a whole series of important rights. They have substantial access to education, work, and personal and family autonomy, although the daily mass media does not allow us to be over-complacent: women are too often the victims of elective violence. There are even new forms of slavery – increasingly evident in city streets in which women from the poorest areas of the planet are victimized. In these cases, the very idea of a Western society benevolent towards women seems to have sunk almost without trace. The fact that we may decide complacently not to impose our way of seeing things on the members of other cultures does not mean that we are entitled to shirk all responsibility for what happens on our own doorsteps.

Those who wish to keep immigrants in a limbo of dubious rights and duties consign the weakest members of these populations to a squalid system of bargaining, blackmail and illegality. The face which our society shows to foreigners is often that of the back-street landlord who rents out shoddy, dirty accommodation for exorbitant sums, the office worker who hands over officially requested and rightfully acquired documents in exchange for surreptitious cash, and the client of the child prostitute. These faces do not help members of other cultures to orient themselves in our world. We say "orient themselves" and not "become integrated" because integration is often perceived, particularly by minorities in the United States and many European countries, as defeat, as yielding to a system of extraneous values, and it is therefore rejected by increasing numbers of people who refuse to abjure their traditions.

What happens during the course of contacts between members of different cultures is not usually integration, but a series of processes of social influence which ramify in various directions, not only from the top downwards. All cultural systems realize they are incomplete, needing the contribution of others, even when those others are deemed to be untrustworthy or inferior (Grinker, 1990, 1994). Perhaps, therefore, it is more appropriate to speak of hybridization to describe what happens during close contacts between peoples from various areas of the planet. The new environments of electronic communication which connect sometimes remote social and cultural groups might favour the kind of identity shift which befell Alvar Nuñez, who became a shaman among the Indians after leaving Spain as a *conquistador*.

SEXUAL (AND OTHER) MUTILATIONS

Some important cultural differences – *à propos*, for example, of women's condition – are now making their appearance in Western countries. France, Italy and the United Kingdom report cases of sexual mutilation of women with consternation. Such practices, traditionally imposed on women "for their own good", are widespread in Somalia, Eritrea, the Sudan and Egypt, and extend as far as Ghana, Senegal and Nigeria (Dorkenoo, 1994), involving about two hundred million women. Many of these, who have immigrated into European countries, try to use the health services of their host countries not only to be treated for the consequences of their mutilations but sometimes even to ask for the same practices for their daughters. They wish their daughters, when they return to their own country, to marry and have normal families, in which case those daughters must be "circumcised" as tradition prescribes.

Female sexual mutilations, which some blandly call "circumcision", are of two types. One is simple excision of the clitoris. The other is infibulation, which involves removal of the clitoris followed by removal of the large and small lips of the vulva. The surrounding tissues are then sewn together, leaving only a small hole for the passage of urine and menstrual blood. An ethological explanation for the origin of these practices has been advanced (Grassivaro Gallo and Viviani, 1992). Their consequences are drastic: infections are common, genital inflamation frequent, and sexual intercourse often painful. In some countries, these customs are justified because women are believed to be sexually insatiable and their desire must be kept under rigorous control if they are not to bring dishonour upon themselves and their families.

In 1996, a video showing excision of the clitoris carried out in a private house in Egypt was shown by the CNN television network and watched by millions of appalled spectators throughout the world. The publicity given to the affair allowed two young Nigerian girls, who had just escaped from their country and their relatives in order to avoid mutilation, to take refuge in the United States – asylum which had initially been refused by officials who were not sufficiently acquainted with the problem. Western countries prohibit by law this kind of mutilation; but the question cannot be resolved merely by prohibitions, which can be sometimes circumvented, or even by harsh sentences inflicted on transgressors as happened in some European countries in 1998 and 1999. A change in mentality is required; for this we can count on processes of social influence in people who dwell on the boundaries between different cultures. For Somali and Nigerian women living in Western countries, a transformation in their attitudes towards female sexual mutilations becomes less difficult when they realize that return to their original country will be consistently delayed.

Traditional cultures are not necessarily cruel, although in many cases they appear less sensitive than modern Western cultures to the need to avoid physical pain. In traditional societies, physical suffering often plays an important role in controlling emotions. Let us consider the following episode, taken from the report by Norman Lewis (1993) of his stay with the Dani of Irian Jaya, part of New Guinea now belonging to Indonesia. The village chief's favourite wife, an old lady called Acu, keeps her hands behind her, in order to hide the fact that she is lacking most of her fingers. Later, overcoming her shyness, she answers the foreigner's questions:

NL: How did you come to lose your fingers?

ACU: I had four cut off when my grandfather died. That left only two for my father. I don't know how old I was. I was just a very young girl.

NL: (I had read that it was usual to reduce the pain of such operations by tying the finger with a ligature below the joint to be severed; then immediately before the amputation striking the elbow over the ulnar nerve; I asked if this had been done)

ACU: No, nothing. These four were cut off all at the same time. Like this . . . One by one they were cut off. My grandfather was a very good man and I loved him, so they cut off my fingers. When he died I put my hand on a piece of wood like this, then one by one they were cut off. This was done because I was sad, and to appease the ancestors.

NL: What was used to remove the fingers?

ACU: A little stone axe. With this they chopped and no one held me.

NL: But Acu, you have lost your ears. What happened?

ACU: We are only allowed to lose six fingers, so when my grandmother died I gave an ear for her. I took a bamboo knife and with this I cut off one ear. The other I cut off when they stole my pig. This was a pig I loved, so I lost my ear.

(Lewis, 1993: 253–4)

In the sequence of mutilations which punctuate the course of her life, Acu seems to have found an effective way of coping with her grief. Counting her missing fingers and ears she can contain and express both her ancient mourning for her grandfather's death and her recent pain and protest for the theft of her beloved pig.

Chapter 6

So near and yet so far

THE CALL OF GOD AND CONSCIENCE

The figures of Alvar Nuñez and Robinson Crusoe are the two poles between which revolves that process of re-interpretation of our own identity which often accompanies encounters with different symbolic worlds. On one hand, some cultural differences are so profound that people cannot even begin to understand the actions of others and are both awed and confused, as Helms was when he watched the three courageous Balinese women celebrating *suttee*. But what happens when people, despite their bewilderment, are obliged to take up positions, choose one side or another in a conflict? How is it that we are able to make decisions even when we are torn between baffling feelings or contrasting identities, as happened to Alvar Nuñez, Spaniard and Indian at one and the same time?

When Robinson Crusoe saw the band of cannibals disembarking on his island and preparing for their gory feast, he immediately planned to attack them. But then, as if he had read a present-day cultural anthropology textbook and been convinced by the author's arguments in favour of the protection of differences, he changed his mind and decided not to interfere with local customs.

> I do not mean that I entertained any fear of their numbers; for as they were naked, unarmed wretches, 'tis certain I was superior to them; Nay, though I had been alone; but it occurred to my thoughts, what call, what occasion, much less what necessity I was in to go and dip my hands in blood, to attack people who had neither done, or intended me any wrong, who as to me were innocent, and whose barbarous customs were their own disaster, being in them a token indeed of God's having left them, with the other nations of this part of the world, to such stupidity, and to such inhumane courses.
>
> (Defoe, 1719 [1972]: 232)

Crusoe's attitude reflects a crystal-clear line of moral reasoning: being a cannibal is not a praiseworthy thing, but it is not up to him to correct the practices of traditional societies in their own territories. "[God] did not call me to take upon me to be a judge of their actions, much less an executioner of His justice; that whenever He thought fit, He would take the cause into His own hands, and by national vengeance punish them as a people, for national crimes; but that in the mean time, it was none of my business" (Defoe, 1719 [1972]: 233). So Crusoe decides to creep up and observe their barbarous feast but not to intrude, unless something involving a divine call and his conscience intervene. Hidden near the beach where the cannibals are holding their banquet, he sends Friday ahead to reconnoitre. All of a sudden Friday returns to Crusoe and reports that:

They were all about their fire, eating the flesh of one of their prisoners; and that another lay bound upon the sand, a little from them, which he said they would kill next, and which fired all the very soul within me; he told me it was not one of their nation, but one of the bearded men, who he had told me of, that came to their country in the boat. I was filled with horror at the very naming of the white bearded man, and going to the tree, I saw plainly by my glass a white man who lay upon the beach of the sea, with his hands and his feet ty'd, with flags, or things like rushes; and that he was an European, and had clothes on.

(Defoe, 1719 [1972]: 233)

At this point, Crusoe abandons his idea of not interrupting the hideous banquet. The situation has precipitated and an appeal has been made to his innermost sense of duty – that of saving a white man, a European, a Christian, a man like himself. "One of us", he might have said. There is no need to wait for God to pronounce judgement on the crime about to be perpetrated before his very eyes. God has already expressed his will by sending Crusoe to that spot at that moment. He is the scourge of God uplifted to strike evil-doers. The divine call has come and it is unequivocal. His surprise attack, narrated with the quick tempo of a film sequence, is fast, effective and lethal.

I turned to Friday. "Now, Friday," said I, "do as I bid thee"; Friday said he would; "Then, Friday," says I, "do exactly as you see me do, fail in nothing"; so I set down one of the muskets and the following-piece upon the ground, and Friday did the like by his; and with the other musket I took my aim of the savages, bidding him to do the like; then asking him if he was ready, he said yes. "Then fire at them, said I"; and in the same moment I fired also. Friday took his aim so much better than I, that on the side that he shot, he killed two of them, and wounded three more; and on my side I killed one, and wounded two. They were, you might be sure, in a dreadful consternation.

(Defoe, 1719 [1972]: 234)

The one-sided battle over, Crusoe counts the dead. Thanks to his boldness, the help of his faithful servant Friday and his superior technology, of the twenty-one savages intent on their gruesome meal only four manage to escape, retreating in disorder to the canoes in which they had arrived so confidently. All the others have been killed by the reluctant Crusoe. His intervention leads to the freeing of the bearded Spaniard and also of Friday's father who, we are informed at this point, had also been singled out for inclusion on the menu.

FROM TOLERANCE TO INTERVENTION

The success of his bloody operation conferred enormous power on Crusoe. He was now absolute sovereign of a territory and of other human beings:

> My island was now peopled, and I thought myself very rich in subjects; and it was a merry reflection which I frequently made, how like a king I looked. First of all, the whole country was my own property; so that I had an undoubted right of dominion. Secondly, my people were perfectly subjected: I was absolute lord and lawgiver; they all owed their lives to me, and very ready to lay down their lives, if there had been occasion of it, for me. It was remarkable too, we had but three subjects, and they were of three different religions. My man Friday was a Protestant, his father was a pagan and a cannibal, and the Spaniard was a Papist. However, I allowed liberty of conscience throughout my dominions.
>
> (Defoe, 1719 [1972]: 240–1)

His benevolent regime cannot blind us to the fact that he describes the most frequently accepted justifications made by European colonial enterprises for their actions. The original idea was that conquest and conversion to Christianity were spiritually beneficial for natives because, although with a certain degree of uncouthness, they led to their eternal salvation. When this concept began to acquire a somewhat tarnished aspect, the Europeans developed a new version of the redemption they were bringing "barbarous" peoples, this time civil rather than religious. Despite this subtle change, it is difficult to appreciate the humanitarian aspect of episodes such as the opium war waged by the British from 1839 to 1842 in order to obtain recognition of their sacrosanct right to introduce opium by the ton into China, despite prohibition by the local authorities. Nor can we entirely ignore the heavy aerial bombardment with toxic gases which the Italians (home-loving lads, all spaghetti, pizza and romantic Neapolitan serenades) inflicted on Ethiopia in 1936 as part of an attempt to create an anachronistic, bloody and short-lived empire.

Crusoe might have found other examples of no less inhuman cruelty than that of his cannibals: in 1692, in the city of Salem, Massachusetts, Puritans like himself unleashed a ruthless witch-hunt, not hesitating to inflict on the weaker members of their community the very persecutions which had originally led them to leave their native country. But God's call did not guide Crusoe to the well-ordered and well-guarded New England, but to the remote island at the mouth of the Orinoco on which Defoe had shipwrecked him. In any case, it was generally easier to force civilization on savages at the end of a musket rather than on pious and obstinate Puritans. We may wonder how was it that, after having decided to leave the cannibals in peace, Crusoe then changed his mind and attacked them with all his strength.

The answer is clear: he had seen a white European, a man like himself, in danger. A mechanism was triggered which led him to identify himself with the member of his group and to defend him from his enemies. Social psychologists have studied the development of intergroup relations and linked them to processes of social identity construction (Tajfel, 1981; Tajfel and Turner, 1986). Crusoe's dramatic change in attitude, from tolerance to armed intervention ending in bloodshed, offers us a vivid example of how ingroup–outgroup processes work. In situations in which a member of the group we feel we belong to is at risk we feel obliged, out of a sense of duty which touches us as the recipients of the call of God and conscience, to intervene, to defend both our kin and our system of values. The consequence of this basic group process is that we can tolerate the existence of concepts and values in conflict with our principles only if they are applied outside our own world, in ways which do not threaten our identity, our habits and our friends.

What decent European would have abandoned another European to a bunch of bloodthirsty cannibals simply in order not to interfere with their ancestral rites? If there is a common space where the other intends to apply his ways of doing things but where we too believe we have the right to affirm ours; and if those principles are mutually incompatible, then conflict becomes inevitable, provided that both we and the others are decent members of our respective societies and therefore ready to do our duty to defend them. Robinson Crusoe attacked the savages not because he was a violent man, but because he was obeying the laws of his culture. If he had not done so, he would not have been a gentle human being but a despicable individual unworthy of anyone's respect. Cultural conflicts may trigger violent encounters which have the character of moral obligations for all their members.

Distance, both physical and symbolic, often creates a barrier against the arousal of destructive feelings between groups. What happens when distance is reduced almost to nothing and two cultures fight over the same territory, the same holy places and even the same patriarchs? The tormented area we call Israel, Palestine or the Holy Land is a good example. Here, distance cannot act as a safety valve because the conflicting parties live on top of each other, each convinced that the others are essentially usurping their birth-right. Here the cultural conflict appears in all its harshness and leaves only two escape routes open: a shared framework for coexistence and cohabitation, if not of peace; or an endless escalation of intransigence, recrimination and vengeance.

The same territories, cities and places are claimed as non-negotiable by groups who consider each other to be mutually hostile (although this has not always been the case in the past). El Kuds, the Moslem name for Jerusalem, is the third holy city of Islam, after Mecca and Medina. It was from here that, so Moslems believe, one night the Prophet ascended into heaven. Omar's Mosque, the Dome of the Rock, completed in AD 691, and the near-by mosque of El Aqsa, built on the spot from which Mohammed began his journey, have been holy places for devout Moslems for many centuries.

On exactly the same spot, in the past rose the temple of Solomon, contain-ing the Holy Tabernacle, the fundamental element in the historical and religious identity of the Jewish people. Of the temple, destroyed by the Roman emperor Titus in AD 70 after a great Jewish revolt, only the western buttress now remains, part of the wall which supported the embankment on which the temple was originally built. For centuries, this wall of squared stone has been a place of pilgrimage for Jews, who come to it to remember, to pray, and to mourn the dispersion of their people, the persecutions which have afflicted past generations and the victims of the *Shoah*. This is not the moment to discuss the interest which holy places have for Christians – not because it is of lesser importance than for the other two religions, but simply because at the present time Christians are not making strong territorial claims on these areas like those which have led to the violent conflict which now flares between Palestinian Moslems and Israeli Jews.

MODEL STUDENTS

We could simply shrug our shoulders and say that these are not cultural problems but the usual run-of-the-mill political conflicts, fully comprehen-sible in terms of local events (the various Arab/Israeli wars, the Palestinian refugee problem, etc.) and international equilibria (rivalry between two blocs, Arab nationalism, Zionism, Gulf oil, etc.), but this is not the case. Let us consider a typical episode. At 6.25 a.m. on 3 May 1996, an Islamic kamikaze terrorist set off his bomb on Jaffa Road, Jerusalem, inside an ordinary red-and-white number 8 bus, the same line which had been the object of a lethal attack the previous week. His action killed 18 passengers, almost all of whom were travelling to work, and injured many other people.

The young man responsible for this horrible crime (according to the Israeli authorities and most people in the world) or this martyr dying in a good cause (according to the supporters of his terrorist group) was called Islam Mohammad. He was 24, went to the mosque five times a day to pray and listen to the preachers, and was a model student at the University of Bir Zeid, the same university at which young men responsible for other terrorist attacks had studied, including Yahja Ayyash, known as "Engineer Death" by the Israelis for having organized devastating kamikaze bomb attacks on civilians over the previous months. Islam's bomb was intended to revenge the killing of Ayyash by the Israeli secret services.

What prompted this devout young man to wreak his terrible revenge? According to the mass media, he had been greatly struck by the Hebron massacre, in which one of his relatives had died. Islam's family did come from Hebron, at that time occupied by the Israelis. Hebron is the city which holds the Tombs of the Patriarchs, places holy for Jews and Moslems alike, where members of both religions go to pray – separately, in order to avoid the kind of confrontation which had already taken place in the past. In spite of rigorous security measures, on 25 February 1994, a member of the Hebron kibbutz, Dr Baruch Goldstein, armed to the teeth, managed to enter the room reserved for Moslems in the Tombs of the Patriarchs and, in circumstances which have never been properly clarified, killed 21 people and wounded many more.

Dr Goldstein was immediately killed by the Israeli security forces and, like the kamikaze Moslems before and after him, was considered a martyr by his companions. These included many members of his kibbutz, politicians who were trying to resolve the Palestinian question by force of arms, and various fundamentalist rabbis who were not willing to share the land promised by God to the Jews with intruders who had only arrived thirteen centuries before. The reckoning of the victims of opposing causes, the restoration of Israel within its confines in the time of King David, or its destruction by Palestinian militants, all draw us into a vortex of endless acts of revenge.

Universities and temples may serve as schools of violence not only for Palestinians. Yigal Amir, the young man who killed the Israeli premier Rabin in order to block the peace process in Palestine, was also a model student. He had gone to a Jewish university, Bar-Ilan, founded in 1955 on the outskirts of Tel Aviv and a stronghold of fundamentalism. Yigal's teachers knew him as a serious, sensitive intellectual who spent most of his time studying the *halacha* under the guidance of highly esteemed masters. From them he learnt that the *Torah* requires Jews to annihilate those who wish to destroy them as a people, in a kind of *ante litteram* anti-*jihad*. He put into practice what he had learnt and declared in court that he had simply done his duty: a Jew who, like Rabin, "gives over his people and his land to the enemy, must be killed. My whole life has been spent studying the *halacha* and I have all the *data*".

David Hartmann, an Orthodox rabbi from Jerusalem, bitterly commented that Rabin's killer was

an innocent, straight kid who took his tradition seriously or too literally. Not only did he hear what secular politicians had to say about the
peace process, he heard from his Orthodox rabbis the powerful language of religious dogmatism. And it was often couched in the absolute
formulas articulated in the *halacha* by rabbis under the radically different conditions prevailing during the third century AD. These texts the
killer absorbed became his identity. They encouraged hate and destruction. Amir was no aberration. He was wholly *within* the normative
tradition that has survived frozen through the ages to our own age.

(Elon, 1995: 42)

The inquiry into Rabin's murder, says Elon,

brought into the open the seedy underworld of ruthless terrorists
informally allied with fairly prominent religious leaders, rabbis, mysta-
gogues, kabbalists, and other salvation-mongers. Everybody who follows public events knew of, or suspected, the existence of this
underworld. For years its exponents had been talking their heads off in
the local and foreign press. Yet in the past hardly anybody in power had
been willing to deal with them seriously, perhaps because they had
mostly threatened only Arabs in the Occupied Territories. To the extent
that a few right-wing terrorists had been prosecuted in the past, they
had, as a rule, been treated leniently by the courts.

(Elon, 1995: 42)

Even when those responsible for violence were condemned to various
kinds of punishment, the sentences were commuted and the prisoners soon
set free. Elon writes that this happened

to the different groups of terrorists who, in 1983, murdered three students at Hebron's Islamic College, crippled two Arab mayors, and con-
spired to blow up the Dome of the Rock on the Temple Mount of
Jerusalem. According to a report submitted to the Attorney General in
the late 1980s, hundreds of suspected acts of aggression by settlers
against Palestinians remained unresolved, including several killings and
numerous instances in which Palestinians have been wounded or
beaten. Since then, there have been many more.

(Elon, 1995: 42)

The script is unchanged, because those who clash on the terrain of terror-
ism are all the same. They all reason in the same way. They depend on each
other to justify their very existence.

THE THREE RINGS

Terrorist groups make war on those who do not share their logic of com-
pulsive murder and spiralling revenge: children celebrating carnival, house-
wives going shopping, office workers getting up at crack of dawn in order to
reach their offices on time. Violent enterprises meet with general although
not universal consensus. Half the students of the schools of Gaza, Bethlehem
and Hebron did not take part in the demonstrations organized by the Palestinian authorities to deplore Islam's massacre of 3 May 1996. Some young
people answered the questions of Western reporters saying that, although
from a humanitarian point of view they were sorry to see so many civilians,
often young people like themselves, brutally killed, politically they understood the fight that Hamas was conducting. Terrorists were considered
martyrs sacrificing themselves for the Palestinian people.

These are not irresponsible young men. In the mosques of Palestine, wrote
the international press, a *fatwa* was proclaimed, a decree issued by the
Islamic religious authorities, prohibiting the faithful even from shaking
hands with Israelis or buying anything from them. When families, school
teachers and religious authorities give young people such directives we are
clearly dealing with social and cultural processes rather than with individual
crimes. The influence of culture makes its presence felt at the moments
and in the places where people learn the rules of life which make them
responsible members of their communities. At every new terrorist attempt,
governments respond by setting aside funds for even more sophisticated
weaponry, ever more sensitive bomb detectors, increasingly penetrating
intelligence. Perhaps they would be wiser to focus their attention on what
happens in educational environments, which form, and inform, the values
which people follow, with greater or lesser consistency, in their everyday
lives.

We are unfortunately little familiar to reason in terms of culture, because
we have neglected this dimension for too long. Terrorist actions are organized in secret, but their cultivation is the most manifest, most public and
most highly institutionalized we can imagine. University professors,
religious leaders and ambitious politicians may contribute towards turning
an "innocent, straight kid" into a cold-blooded assassin. The uses to which
some groups put religion remind us of the warning of Primo Levi (1989:
193): "As it is difficult to distinguish true prophets from false ones, it is
better to suspect all prophets. It is better to renounce revealed truths, even
though their simplicity and splendour excite us, even though we find them
convenient because they are acquired free of charge".

Avoiding fanaticism is not enough. We must break down the barriers
which hatred has erected over the years and which are now part and parcel
of the memory of communities at war for too long. In Medieval Europe, in
order to inspire a certain religious tolerance, a story which Boccaccio (the

great Tuscan writer of fourteenth-century Italy, inventor of the modern novel) has handed down to us, was sometimes told. The words are those of his character, Filomena, on the first of the ten days of the *Decameron*. The story goes that, in order to seize for himself the riches of the Jew Melkisedek, the Sultan asks him which of the three laws, Saracen, Hebrew or Christian, he believes is the true law. Melkisedek avoids the trap by narrating the following story.

A great lord, he says, had decreed that a magnificent ring was to be given to the son chosen to be his heir. The precious ring, the sign of favour, thus passed from generation to generation until it reached a father who had three sons, "all handsome, virtuous, and obedient to their father's wishes, so that he loved them all equally". The father, unable to favour one son against his brothers, resorted to a stratagem: he had two more rings made, identical to the first, and presented them secretly to each of his three sons. Later, this father's love was to cause great strife, since each of the sons was convinced he was the favourite and claimed the entire inheritance which he believed was due to him from his father.

Yet it was not hatred but the equal love the father bore his three sons that lay at the root of their division. It is the idea that there is only a single favourite which turns brothers into enemies: on this premise, not even the loving father's trick was able to overcome the rivalry which broke out. In another context, this basic truth was also perceived by an extraordinary figure of our times, Ingrid Warburg, born in Hamburg in 1910 into a Jewish banking family. In 1936, she emigrated to the United States where, in the middle of the war, she married an Italian, Veniero Spinelli, a poor but courageous man, a staunch opposer of Fascism. Ingrid, a woman who dared to commit herself to the struggle against evil at a terrible moment in the history of the world, wrote in her memoirs: "I was convinced that the idea of the Chosen People was wrong – that is, I thought 'God's People' meant everyone" (Warburg Spinelli, 1990).

Inheritance belongs either to everybody or to nobody. This should now be accepted as an obvious moral, political and ecological fact, in a world in which the fates of all of us are increasingly entwined. Together with grim episodes in the relationships among different cultures we also find bright moments full of light and warmth, like the scene which Warburg Spinelli describes at the end of her book. A group of women taking part in a demonstration for peace in Northern Ireland had agreed to meet on the banks of a river. At first, recalls Warburg Spinelli, nothing could be seen. "Thick fog covered everything. No-one knew how many women would have the courage to come. Suddenly the fog lifted and thousands of women appeared on both banks. They rejoiced, hugged each other, and swore to work together for peace" (Warburg Spinelli, 1990: 213). Sometimes, all of a sudden, the sooty fog of hatred, unexpectedly, lifts and we can see and recognize each other.

Part III

The web of culture

During winter manoeuvres in the Swiss Alps, a Hungarian platoon of soldiers is sent out to reconnoitre. The weather suddenly worsens, with snow, ice and then thick fog. The soldiers do not return either the following day or the one after. On the third day, when the commanding officer is going to give up hope, the entire platoon arrives back safely. They say they had got lost in the fog, had sheltered in a cave for two days, and on the third had found their way back to camp with the aid of a map one of them had with him. The officer asks to see it, and discovers that it is a map of the Pyrenees. The story is reported by Karl Weick (1995), of the University of Michigan, in his book on sense-making, which analyses people's capability to orient themselves in unforeseen, unprecedented and often potentially dangerous situations.

The anecdote of the lost platoon shows that, in order to find our way in the contingencies of daily life, we need not only the right instruments but, particularly, the capacity to use them flexibly: even a map of another place can sometimes be useful in finding one's way in a difficult situation. Culture is the map we use to structure reality, a map which mediates between individuals and the environment, enveloping them in a network of sense. Culture is not an instrument of homogenization, as if it were a mould making us all alike. On the contrary, it is precisely culture which acknowledges and enhances human differences.

Chapter 7, *Sun counters*, examines culture as a sense-making activity. Thanks to a network of analogies, culture links different domains of reality. At the same time, it supplies its members with a repertoire of shared beliefs and a sense of one's place in the world. It is this network of sense-making that allows the members of a given society to understand each other and to communicate.

Chapter 8, *Pride and dignity*, is devoted to the most important and least understood function of culture, that of defining values. What is dignity? What must we be proud of? Where is happiness? These are all questions to which every culture attempts to provide answers. The answers vary from one culture to another, and even inside one symbolic system they may be inconsistent, but it is essential that answers be found. Our neglect of the cultural dimension is in part responsible for the eclipse of moral discourse in social sciences. In order to explore the building of shared moral worlds we have to pay attention to the ways in which people choose their models for life and tell stories about what duty, honour, commitment are to be conceived of.

Chapter 9, *The blind man's cane*, deals with the basic, general function of culture: mediation. Artifacts mediate the relationship between the human mind and its environment. They can be physical tools, like a table fork, or ideal tools, like the norms which direct our use of forks during a gala dinner; artifacts are embodied projects. Cultural mediation is an extension of the mind, like the cane which a blind man uses to explore the pavement in front of him. This image from Bateson tells us that the tools we use to interact with the environment are neither *outside* nor *inside* our minds, but in both places. They are interfaces linking our many interests and goals with the various opportunities we can see in our environment.

Chapter 7

Sun counters

HARD AND SOFT FACTS

Over the last century, the social sciences often favoured the study of certain dimensions, believing them to be the mainstays of society. It was believed that they controlled other dimensions, which were thus viewed as derivative. Marxism is an example of this approach: in its orthodox forms, it counterposes the economic structure of society (possession of the means of production, control of the work-force, etc.) with its ideological superstructure (systems of beliefs, art, religion) which is its simple projection. This way of thinking had, and still has, some advantages: it allows us to link the ideas we read about in newspapers with the influence, direct or indirect, which the newspaper owner exercises on the composition of the editorial staff, the careers of its personnel, which journalists to hire, and so on. Similarly, we can understand to some extent how television works, who benefits from the spread of certain ideas and how they can serve the interests of groups which our press, with some servilism, calls "strong powers".

There is no doubt that the economic structure of a society often exerts a considerable influence on the development and circulation of ideas. But there is a great difference between recognizing this fact and thinking that every belief, idea and ritual may be taken back to an economic "core" which contains its hidden truth. The social history of art describes the environment in which certain works of art were produced, but it does not tell us why and how they are works of art: knowing which illustrious family or rich corporation commissioned which artist to create a certain altar-piece does not exhaust our understanding of the work itself. It may be interesting to know why the Scrovegni family, Medieval bankers, wished to cleanse their name from the stain of usury by calling Giotto to Padova to decorate their chapel in the Eremitani church; what political reasons inspired Lorenzo de Medici, in Renaissance Florence, to ask Michelangelo to design and sculpt in the church of San Lorenzo the tombs of his family; and that the need to legitimize an upstart dynasty induced the Farnese family to call the elderly and reluctant Titian to Rome to paint

Pope Paul III on his throne surrounded by his son and grandchildren. But the art of Giotto, Michelangelo and Titian are only obliquely illuminated by the circumstances in which they were commissioned, appreciated and used.

The priority of the economic dimension has also been accepted to a great extent in the psychological research of the last few decades. For example, if differences in the linguistic development of children were studied, it seemed obvious to relate them to the socio-economic conditions of their families, and this did generally turn out to be the case. This was not surprising, since we know that scholars often prefer to follow styles of research aiming at confirming their hypotheses rather than at disproving them, as a rigorously scientific method would require. The fact that the children of poor families used more rudimentary language than those of middle-class ones seemed to confirm the expectations that the economic dimension of society had a predominant influence on child development. In actual fact, the differences were also due to both innate and cultural factors, which were responsible for the relational style of the family, the content and form of communications, and the circle of relatives, friends and acquaintances to which the children were exposed.

Attention to cultural processes is beginning to replace yesterday's grey economic determinism with more sophisticated grids for interpreting reality. We can now appreciate how many important processes depend on the normative social context in which they develop. People do not remain frozen in a carapace of fixed attitudes, but are capable of changing according to both environment and circumstances. My way of behaving with girls while I am out with friends is more lively and cordial than it is when I am out with Anna, who is very jealous and who obliges me to pretend an indifference and a lack of warmth which I do not in fact feel.

People's lives are structured not only by power relations but also by the need to make sense of actions and situations, as Geertz (1995) notes:

> No matter how much one trains one's attention on the supposedly hard facts of social existence, who owns the means of production, who has the guns, the dossiers, or the newspapers, the supposedly soft facts of that existence, what do people imagine human life to be all about, how do they think one ought to live, what grounds belief, legitimizes punishment, sustains hope, or accounts for loss, crowd in to disturb simple pictures of might, desire, calculation, and interest.
>
> (Geertz, 1995: 43)

We have to acknowledge that in everyday life "everyone, everywhere, always, lives in a world permeated with meaning" (Geertz, 1995). The depressing scenario presented to us by the old economic determinism affecting psychological studies is vanishing, to be replaced by a more interesting and lively vision of social reality as a place for rich sense-making processes (Bruner, 1990).

A NETWORK OF ANALOGIES

How does sense-making occur? One answer comes from cognitive scientists Holyoak and Thagard (1995), who work on analogies. They believe that analogies are creative acts, true mental leaps by means of which people establish connections between different domains of reality, connections which are founded on the recognition of similarities. Analogies try to demonstrate how a given reality domain is functioning starting from what we know about another domain we know even better. Constructing an analogy means creating a bridge between two situations, across which we let pass what we have understood of the first in order to discover something which escapes us in the second. We orient ourselves in ambiguous situations by seeking to collocate them in already known categories, whose meaning we have already successfully decoded.

Analogy is a resource as indispensable as it is uncertain. It is widespread, although its validity in single cases is not guaranteed. We can never know *a priori* whether a particular analogy really meets the relevant aspects of a situation. Although we have a potentially infinite network of analogies, in order to apply one to a single case, we are often obliged to force the terms of our problem, as we saw *à propos* the Iraq of Saddam Hussein and the Germany of Adolf Hitler as defined by the mass media during the Gulf War.

In order to orient ourselves in unknown environments, we create links between sometimes very remote areas of reality: how many New Zealands, New South Waleses and New Scotlands arose in far-off seas when European navigators attempted to make sense of their disconcerting adventures to the Antipodes? In their first steps on the soil of the New World, the Europeans exorcised the threat of an alien environment by resorting to that most powerful of symbolisms, religion. The images evoked by such names as Santa Cruz, Santa Fé, San Francisco and Santa Barbara, Nuestra Senora de los Angeles and Sacramento were all exploited to tame wild places and bring them within the mental geography of Christianity. The admiral who called one island after the Saviour (El Salvador) through the same act gave thanks for having been saved from the tempest, marked the date of his disembarkment, and placed the new settlement under the protection of a celestial and familiar power.

According to Holyoak and Thagard (1995), there are three levels in the formation of analogies. On the first level, an analogy is based on the fact that two objects have similar physical attributes. On the second, analogy is based on similarity in the reciprocal relations between the objects present in the two domains in question. On the third level, the analogy captures important structural characteristics that are common to the two domains linked by the analogy itself. Type three analogies require abstract aspects in situations to be identified and compared; this "system mapping" is proper to mature human intelligence and goes beyond the competence of non-human primates and that of children under the age of five.

In reality, things are not always so clearly and sharply defined as in theory. If I say that Anna (why do I keep thinking of the girl?) is "a wren", first-level mapping is certainly present in my analogy, due to several visible attributes: Anna is indeed tiny, like a wren. But my analogy also contains third-level mapping, since categorizations and stereotypes which refer to women and birds form part of the "Anna/wren" parallel that I am establishing. The fragility, fluttering wings and delicacy of a vulnerable little creature like a wren are used by the analogy to reveal, beyond possible physical similarities between Anna and a wren, something which deals with Anna, who actually has a great deal in common with the battleship Potemkin.

Analogies are often of the third type because the similarities which people see are not only physical. And it is here that we find the cultural framework. Third-level analogies are nothing more than those which use links based on similarities drawn from pre-existing symbolic systems. When a Christian says that Christ is the Lamb of God, he does not really think that Christ resembles a normal lamb: he is referring to a similarity of function, that of sacrifice, which he does not invent but which he finds in his religious tradition. The analogy is solemnly transmitted to him in the Easter liturgy and Holy Scripture and, in an even more pervasive form, in images, ways of speech and daily practices.

Culture is made up of a wide, robust web of analogic links:

> The web of culture that holds people together in social groups is constructed from shared beliefs and feelings, knowledge of a common history, and a sense of place in the natural and social world. These strands provide the connections by which members of a society can communicate with one another. Myth and magic, rites and ceremonies, poetry and everyday conversation all form part of the web. A culture is built and maintained in large part by symbolic stories and rituals, in which objects and events are given meanings that in various ways go beyond themselves. Analogy plays a prominent role in providing these extended meanings and thus in building and maintaining the web of culture.
>
> (Holyoak and Thagard, 1995: 211)

THE FABRIC OF REALITY

Let us resort to a definite scenario to see how the web of culture works. Consciousness of our place in the order of things is an essential aspect of sense-making. For the Aztecs, the key to this order was time:

Mythical time had a determining influence on human time in the sense that the coincidence of a moment of human time with one moment of ever-present mythical time determined the very substance of that fleeting instant. These meetings followed complex cycles of variable amplitude, whose combinations structured human time. It was the meeting of these cycles which governed the order of arrival of the benevolent or malevolent forces acting on the individual, who was submitted from birth to hidden superior forces controlling his destiny.

(Gruzinski, 1988: 24)

The outcome of any initiative, whether a war or a wedding, depended on knowing these cycles and being able to exploit them:

"In order to dominate divine forces, share or contrast them, it was necessary to watch for their first manifestations and prepare an arsenal of practices aimed at the survival of everyone. This was the role of the 'sun counters', the *tonalpouhque*: their wisdom and their *pinturas* oriented all human activities, war, trade, crafts, agriculture, rites of passage and alliance. 'Everything,' they said, 'had its computation, its reason, and its special day.'"

(Gruzinski, 1988: 24)

For the Aztecs, the figures of the sun counters represented the highest form of order and control over the environment that they could imagine. The 'sun counters' were entrusted with tasks that, in our present-day world, would be assigned to scientists and technicians. Their wisdom was power, and people tried to bend their destiny to their own desires with the aid of the *tonalpouhque*. They were able, for example, if a child were born under an evil sign, to choose a favourable day on which to give him a name, thus changing his collocation in cyclical time and consequently mutating his destiny. In the same way, by acting on the divine order of things, the sun counters could control harvests, unleash wars, heal sick persons, or prohibit some weddings.

The sun counters manipulated the strands which held things together. They did not link in their minds domains of the real world which remained separate in reality, as we believe we do when we create our analogies. They acted on forces which, to the uninitiated, seemed to belong to separate domains of reality but which, as the sun counters knew, were only parts of the unique weave of the cosmic web that they were able to see and manipulate. The science and technology in which the sun counters were expert were based on something stronger than the mental operations by means of which we link various areas of reality. The correspondences which they saw were more than analogies, they were reality – a reality rooted in theology, because the forces they manipulated were divine.

The ambition of the sun counters to control reality, not mere thought processes, cannot be viewed as strange: the analogies which act as the load-bearing structures of a given culture are usually more than simple comparisons. Michelle Rosaldo (1984) writes: "Culture is a matter less of artifacts and propositions, rules, schematic programs, or beliefs, than of associative chains and images that suggest what can reasonably link up with what. . . . Culture, far more than a mere catalogue of rituals and beliefs, is instead the very stuff of which our subjectivities are created" (Rosaldo, 1984: 140). The web of analogies on which a culture is founded is not the result of individual options. It describes a state of things, divine and human, shared by whole communities – sometimes vast, as in the case of religious traditions which have been handed down by millions of people throughout the world for generations. Michelle Rosaldo clearly sees this when she states that "meaning is a fact of public life".

Space too occupies an important place in the web of sense-making which envelops people's everyday lives. The Mexican Indios

> believed that the most important mountain peaks and the highest sierras were part of the divinity, and that lakes, caves and mountains were privileged points of contact between the domain of the gods and the surface of the earth. They were the channels which linked the ever-present time of the gods and of the eternal world with that of men, they were passages which could be exploited by the divine powers, and also by men and shamans. Shamans were often described as being puzzled at having reached the earth's surface at a moment they had not expected.
>
> (Gruzinski, 1988: 121)

We have seen in the previous section that objects, as tools of human activity, contain quotas of distributed human knowledge. The considerations made here on one hand exalt the role of natural realities (but the Indios did not consider as "natural" rivers, lakes, caves and mountains which, rather, appeared to them as divine manifestations) in the management of knowledge and, on the other, somehow subvert the sense of our comments on artifacts. For the Indios, natural realities were important not as tools for human plans but as aims in themselves, sacred truths that individuals and communities venerated and from which they derived knowledge and comfort. They were elements of the landscape which transferred to the human mind part of their intrinsic knowledge and power, not vice versa.

The Aztec vision of the landscape is an eloquent example of how culture intervenes in sense-making processes.

> Like an immense, indestructible web, the landscape and the names of the places maintained the memory of an inevitable presence, reflected in the indigenous understanding of the profound nature of the places and

of the meaning of their names. Everywhere, place-names concealed cosmogony, being inseparable from them. For many Indios, a mountain or a spring were not just the material and ephemeral scenario of a superstitious fable: they were endowed with unmeasurable density – sensitive, affective, even sonorous. They still bore the signs of that terrifying presence, that *tetzahuitl*, so closely linked with the autochthonous perception of the divinity.

(Gruzinski, 1988: 122–3)

What was true for the Indios then is true for us now, with a few small differences. We cannot be surprised at the sacred character of the landscape as perceived by the Aztecs, if we reflect on the holy places of apparently sophisticated Western societies: Hollywood, with its now partially disused studios, its stars' footprints immortalized in the cement of sidewalks, its tourists lining up to pay homage to unforgettable events in the history of the cinema; or Marlboro Country, with its grandiose scenery consecrated in a thousand westerns, all duly quoted by the guides, where visitors may be forgiven if they no longer know if they are crossing "real" deserts or are in an armchair at home, watching *The Searchers* or *Red Shadows*.

The same applies to Las Vegas, San Francisco, New York, Hong Kong, Paris, London, Venice, Rome – each with its halo of glorious or squalid myths (Moscow is a special case, after having been "mythical" too in its own chilling way). Even the ski slopes or race tracks of the world's champions, the football stadiums and those fairs of industrial sport called the Olympic Games, they all have their own holy spaces, sacred to the religion of success which, through the media, offers its frustrated adepts scenarios which are only slightly different from the terrifying ones of the Aztec religion. For the adepts of mass media, the new religion, the only truly frightening prospect is not appearing on television.

THE CONFINES OF THE WORLD

The sense of things which is experienced within a given community is crystallized and transmitted mainly through its language. Of all the instruments of mediation, language is the most powerful: we think, communicate and act according to modes defined by the linguistic structures available to us. Geertz (1995), describing his researches in Java and Morocco, notes that understanding of these cultures "came to him" when he began to speak *in situ* the language of the inhabitants. He then realized that the two cultures had different priorities: in Java, the most important thing was status; in Morocco, attention focused on gender. Geertz writes:

In studying Javanese, my instructors insistently and meticulously corrected any errors I made in status marking while letting gender errors more or less go, while my Moroccan instructors – like the Javanese, as university students, hardly traditionalists – never let a gender mistake pass uncorrected and seemed hardly interested in status marking, such of it as there was. It didn't seem to matter, or matter very much, whether you got sex right in Javanese so long as you kept rank straight. In Moroccan, getting genders crossed seemed almost dangerous; certainly it made my teachers, all of them men, as indeed were the Javanese, very nervous. But rank hardly came into consideration at all.

(Geertz, 1995: 46)

However, in another sense, language plays a role similar to that of the Aztec landscape, as a place in which superior powers manifest themselves. In this acceptation, language is not limited to transmitting consolidated and socially shared interpretative grids, but defines the very confines of reality. This is evident at moments in which extraneous cultural systems come into conflict, as occurred in the New World at the time of the Spanish conquest. The Indios watched in dismay as their world was invaded by a perception of reality which was so incomprehensible to them that they initially viewed the Spanish monks as the incarnation of the monsters of their Apocalypse, the *tzitzimime*. On their side, missionaries and *conquistadores* considered the native divinities as nothing less than manifestations of Satan.

Attempts to reduce the distances inevitably failed, due to the incompatible attributions of meaning made by each of the two societies, Indio and Spanish.

How was it possible to make the people understand, show them beings, divine figures, representations of the 'beyond', without equivalents in the native languages and in the local representations, without resorting to approximations which betrayed both substance and form? Everything combined to create misunderstanding: the nahua word *Mictlàn* chosen to represent the Christian hell was, for the Aztecs, just one of the places in which the dead stayed for a time, and in any case for them it was a place of snow and ice; the word used for the Christian paradise, *Ilhuicatl*, had little in common with the native empyrean and its thirteen levels; *In tloque in nahuaque*, 'the Lord of that which is near and that which is far', an expression which the missionaries had chosen for God, originally designated *Ometeotl*, the Lord of Duality, of whom *Tetzalipoca* and *Quetzalcoatl* were only two of the many manifestations. *Tonantzin*, the name assigned to the Virgin Mary, previously indicated one of the forms of the god-mother.

(Gruzinski, 1988: 236)

The obstacles were truly insurmountable. The missionaries used European linguistic and conceptual categories which were incomprehensible to the Indios. When they decided instead to borrow words and images from the Indio world, they could not prevent the ancient gods from continuing to exist in those words and images. The encounters, exchanges and hybridization which were to occur in the subsequent centuries, after much bloodshed, torment and violence, cannot allow us to forget that the price paid for this incompatibility was extremely high: one century after the Spanish conquest, more than 95 per cent of the population of pre-Columbian Mexico had perished.

The webs spun by cultures define reality at the moment when they give it meaning. The Church and the Indios did not define the same limits for reality. The Christian Church excluded certain states (dreams, hallucinations, drunkenness) which took on particular significance in the native cultures. While the Indio society put great emphasis on interpreting dreams, the Church censured such interpretations, declaring them to be senseless, in the same way that it condemned the use of hallucinogenic substances, sources "of alienation, visions and delirium" opening the way to "folly and lust", and denounced every form of drunkenness, including in the same condemnation rituals and sacred forms close to ecstasy and possession.

The idea of culture as a web of meaning offers us a precious occasion to reflect on the roots of cultural differences: what else could the sixteenth-century Catholic Church in the New World do but affirm its vision of reality, when faced with a native religion which, in its view, was nothing less than diabolical? The linguistic and conceptual resources of every culture define the range of experiences on which they are able to confer meaning. They are maps of territories in which some elements are highlighted, others omitted, yet others prohibited. At the present time, when Western societies are becoming increasingly multi-cultural and multi-lingual, we must ask ourselves how we can avoid repeating the forms of open or surreptitious intolerance which prevailed in the past.

Chapter 8

Pride and dignity

THE REALM OF NON-ORDER

We have explored until now two functions of culture, mediating between people and their environment, and giving meaning to reality. There is a third function: motivating people, indicating the goals at which they should aim. Culture undertakes this task not by means of a set of prescriptions, but by proposing concrete models which people can use to clarify the situations in front of them and to find their proper place within their community. Important, life-committing decisions – choosing a job, getting married, having children – are not taken at the end of a rational calculation of expected costs and benefits, but according to an assessment of the desirability of a certain result and the opportunities that a certain action offers, given the circumstances of the moment and the aims of the people involved.

Cost/benefit calculations play a limited role in the intuitive decisions we make every day. How can I measure the effects of processes which are not in themselves quantifiable and which might manifest their effects in the distant future? How can I calculate the attraction exerted on me by Anna's curiosity and determination? What would happen if these brilliant characteristics, which I find fascinating at this moment in time, should become unbearable tomorrow? I would have to redo all my calculations. Or change the headings in my ledger, substituting "pertness" for "curiosity" and "obstinacy" for "determination". The truth is that, not only do I not know what Anna will be like in ten years' time, I can't even imagine what *I* will be like, and I am far from certain that my likes and dislikes will be the same. In these conditions, how on earth can we start thinking of getting married?

And yet, every day, people do get married, choose a faculty, or start a new job. They do these things after pondering over them carefully, but this is not true calculation, since what is considered primarily is if a certain line of action is appropriate or not to the situation and to the current goals of the actors involved in the decision process. Every culture provides its members with the criteria to make assessments of this type. Each of them tells us what happiness is, what we must be proud of, where beauty lies; this is the point from which people start planning for a decent future. If we think of culture as a set of rules governing people's actions, like Microsoft programs controlling computer operations, our idea of the social world will be decidedly over-simplified. Culture entrusts its values not to abstract systems of rules, but rather to attractive models which capture our imagination. We then desire to emulate those models which embody the most noble, beautiful and lovable qualities we can see in the world.

After contemplating these models, we have a clearer idea of how to move within daily contingencies. Culture supplies a not necessarily consistent repertory of situations which may arise, together with appropriate responses to them, which we use to understand situations and make decisions. As disorder, inconsistency and dissent are part of reality, we need a "polyphonic, almost disharmonic" concept of culture, one which does not efface those "traces, ambiguities, contingencies, fragments" (Geertz, 1995) which are the salt of everyday experience. Culture is not a set of norms, a computer program, or a principled order which makes people belonging to the same group all the same. As Renato Rosaldo observes, "Social analysis should look beyond the dichotomy of order versus chaos towards the less explored real of 'nonorder'" (Rosaldo, 1989: 102–3).

People adapt flexibly to situations, and every time they are faced with unexpected circumstances, they resort to their most precious ability, improvisation. Facing a continuously changing world, "People can even plan to improvise by saying that they'll take things as they come, go one step at a time, or play it by ear. Their improvisations can be earnest, playful, or both; their unexpected life events can be joyous, neutral, or catastrophic. A focus on nonorder directs attention to how people's actions alter the conditions of their existence, often in ways they neither intend nor foresee" (Rosaldo, 1989: 102).

Undeniably, behaviour control functions do exist, but this control is more flexible than cognitive theories based on the mind/computer analogy would presume. We should, says Rosaldo, try to

> decenter, not eliminate, the study of control mechanisms. The point is to break abjectivism's monopoly on truth claims, not throw out the baby with the bathwater. In certain respects, after all, cultural practices do conform to codes and norms. People make plans, and sometimes their plans do work out. Not all expectations remain unmet. Conventional wisdom does not always fail. Yet there is more to human culture than the image of cybernetic steering functions suggests.
>
> (Rosaldo, 1989: 102)

THE CHRISTIAN LEOPARD

If we examine closely the forms taken on by the relationship between experience and culture, we generally find not so much true control of culture over
behaviour, as continual tension between traditional beliefs and people's
experiences. Sperber's (1974) studies on the Dorze's beliefs help us to clarify
this point. Sperber lived for a certain period of time with the Dorze, a Coptic
Christian people of farmers dwelling in southern Ethiopia. For the Dorze,
according to unquestioned tradition, the leopard is a Christian animal and,
as such, faithfully respects the numerous fasts required by the Coptic
Church, while the hyena, jackal and other predators are not Christian and
therefore do not respect fasts.

However, Sperber noted that, even on fast days, i.e., Wednesdays and
Fridays, no Dorze relaxed his vigilance in protecting livestock: "It is not that
they suspect that certain leopards are bad Christians; they do not doubt that
they too fast, but leopards are dangerous any day of the week". That is, the
Dorze believe that leopards scrupulously respect fast days and, as a consequence, on Wednesdays and Fridays livestock need not fear them, but the
Dorze know also that in actual fact leopards attack their animals even on
those days, and so they are watchful. The contradiction between the two
statements: "Leopards fast on Wednesdays and Fridays" and "Leopards
hunt every day" is not perceived. Why not?

The fact of the matter is that the Dorze are careful not to pose the question
in these terms. If they did so, they would expose their traditional beliefs to
serious querying. The contradiction which we on the outside see is not evident in Dorze society because "the two statements are never compared. If an
ethnologist insists on questioning a person on this point, that person will
think for a little while and then explain: leopards don't eat the animals they
kill on the fast day, perhaps they eat them the day after" (Sperber, 1974: 93).
But what about the important fasts, which last several weeks? The Dorze
"see in this question an enigma or a problem which must have a solution and
which cannot be weakened in its premises: leopards are always dangerous,
and the Dorze know this by experience; they are Christians, Dorze tradition
ensures it. The Dorze do not seek the solution to this paradox. They simply
know that a solution exists" (Sperber, 1974: 93).

What appears to us to be an evident contradiction – and one which would
be easy to solve by abandoning the idea that the leopard is a Christian
animal – simply appears to the Dorze, who are more interested than we are
in maintaining their traditional beliefs, to be a strange problem, a puzzle,
perhaps difficult but not impossible to solve. Their experience rests confidently on tradition, even when this causes problems: we may recall here the
Dyirbal, for whom birds are the spirits of dead women. Here, for the Dorze,
a tension similar but only slightly stronger than that found among the
Dyirbal arises between experience and tradition. The net of meaning in

which culture envelops reality has holes in it. As such, this is not surprising: all nets have holes in them, that is how they work. The holes must be there, but care must also be taken to see that they do not hinder the development of a normally non-ordered society. The Dorze tolerate latent inconsistencies in *their* belief systems and we are ready to tolerate similar inconsistencies in *our* belief systems.

The webs of meaning that cultures construct are maps which privilege certain aspects of reality at the expense of others. Omissions and imperfections are tolerated as long as they allow the map users to orient themselves safely with respect to their top priorities. Cultural symbolism is an incomplete map, but this allows it to contain those elements of situations which have no place in the mosaic on which our minds are working. Symbolism keeps temporarily unused pieces in a compartment of its memory, awaiting the right moment to insert them in a future, presently unimagined mosaic. Sperber writes:

> The cyclical movement of cultural symbolism would appear absurd unless it represented the constructive character of recall: this is not a desperate search for an impossible solution, but a continually repeated work of reorganization of encyclopedic memory. Every new evocation reconstructs past representations in a different way, entwines new links between them, integrates within the field of symbolism that information which daily life gives us in the present.
>
> (Sperber, 1974: 140)

The Dorze know how to keep at bay the tension which arises in the encounter between people's daily experience, born within the specific context of their living and working community, and traditional beliefs, originally formulated in a different historical context. They preserve the essential feature of symbolism, that of incessantly relaunching an evocation: "They fulfil the same rites, but with new actors; they tell the same myths, but in a changing universe, to people whose social position, relationships with others and experience have been transformed" (Sperber, 1974: 140). Post-modern societies, with their exasperated emphasis on consistency, rationality and cognitive transparency, have little or no tolerance towards the tensions arising between individual experience and cultural transmission.

LOST INNOCENCE

Every culture manages its internal contradictions by means of tacit but extremely efficient acts of suppression. The Dorze have no difficulty in using their webs of meaning and do not allow their latent inconsistencies to worry them, and we do the same, as long as our web serves to organize our lives.

Perhaps the greatest difference lies in the fact that the Dorze do not, for example, travel to Paris to question professors at the Sorbonne about their academic rituals and then highlight their incongruities in erudite scientific papers. Doing things the other way round is easier.

For us, members of Western societies, so certain of our moral superiority, it may be irritating to discover how very questionable some of our traditional beliefs and practices are when challenged by those of other peoples. Renato Rosaldo (1989) tells us of his lost imperialistic innocence in these terms:

> When I was residing in the late 1960s as an ethnographer among the Ilingot of northern Luzon, Philippines, I was struggling against a diffusely overwhelming reaction to one of their central cultural practices: headhunting. Despite my indoctrination in cultural relativism, headhunting seemed utterly alien and morally reprehensible. At the time, I wanted simply to bracket my moral perception in order to carry out the ethnographic project of understanding the practice in its own terms.
>
> (Rosaldo, 1989: 63)

As a conscientious ethnographer, Rosaldo tried to overcome his revulsion at headhunting and to understand what it meant for the Ilingot:

> Early questioning made it appear that headhunting had ended with the last Japanese soldier beheaded in June 1945. These beheadings, Ilingots said, aided the American army. When I asked about more recent headhunting episodes, they indignantly replied, 'How could you think such a thing of us? I helped carry you across a stream. I fed you. I've cared for you. How could you think such a thing?' I could not but agree.
>
> (Rosaldo, 1989: 63)

After staying with the Ilingot for a sufficient period of time, Rosaldo was accepted as a member of their society. A year after his arrival on Luzon, while flying over part of the island with Tukbaw, his brother Ilingot, Tukbaw pointed down and said:

> 'That's where we raided'. He told his American brother that he had gone headhunting there quite recently. Soon everyone began to tell him their headhunting stories and Rosaldo understood that almost every man in the camp had taken a head. He was shocked and disoriented because his companions had indeed been kind to him: how could such caring hosts also be cruel murderers?
>
> (Rosaldo, 1989: 63)

A few months later, Rosaldo was drafted by the US Army for the Vietnam war. But he had no intention of fighting, and waited for his Ilingot friends to disapprove of his decision and believe him to be a coward. Once again he was surprised:

> My companions immediately told me not to fight in Vietnam, and they offered to conceal me in their homes. Though it corresponded to my sentiments, their offer could not have surprised me more. Unthinkingly, I had supposed that headhunters would see my reluctance to serve in the armed forces as a form of cowardice. Instead, they told me that soldiers are men who sell their bodies. Pointedly they interrogated me, 'How can a man do as soldiers do and command his brothers to move into the line of fire?'
>
> (Rosaldo, 1989: 63)

It is easy to see that the American anthropologist and his Ilingot friends were using completely different cultural grids. What was upsetting for Rosaldo was the discovery that a perfectly acceptable Western institution such as war could appear to his Ilingot friends a morally repugnant practice:

> This act of ordering one's own men (one's 'brothers') to risk their lives was utterly beyond their moral comprehension. That their telling question ignored state authority and hierarchical chains of command mattered little. My own cultural world suddenly appeared grotesque. Yet their earnest incomprehension significantly narrowed the moral chasm between us, for their ethnographic observation about modern war was both aggressive and caring. They condemned my society's soldiering at the same time that they urged me not to sell my body.
>
> (Rosaldo, 1989: 63–4)

Rosaldo realized that the headhunters' reaction to modern warfare set him in a new perspective, not only in their view but also in his own:

> I was repositioned through an Ilingot account of one of my culture's central institutions. I could no longer speak as one of the clean addressing the dirty. My loss of innocence enabled me and the Ilingots to face each other on more nearly equal ground, as members of flawed societies. We both lost positions of purity from which to condemn the other, without at the same time having to condone what we found morally reprehensible in ourselves and in the other. Neither war nor headhunting, in deeply serious ways, has been the same for me since.
>
> (Rosaldo, 1989: 64)

When we realize that our values reflect the beliefs of societies which are, in their own ways, far from perfection, the presumption that our ways of thinking are the best ones change drastically. By what right can a Westerner who accepts the planned, technological killing produced by modern warfare – justified by obedience to orders, state authority, and the conviction of a just cause – claim to be morally superior to a headhunter? Is releasing a bomb from an aircraft, killing an unspecified number of people, a praise-worthy gesture, while throwing a spear, killing one person, is not?

MODELS OF DIGNITY

In encounters on the boundaries between cultures, each person easily sees the faults of others' worlds, but understands the defects of his own only slowly and with difficulty. In the end, if everything goes well, the Philippine headhunters and the American anthropologist find themselves closer to one another, but not because they have agreed that homicide is universally prac-tised and so the less fuss made about it, the better. On the contrary, the two sides feel for the practices and beliefs of their own environment, which they had previously accepted, the same disgust they felt when faced with the practices and beliefs of other societies.

The goals which culture suggests are intrinsically gratifying because people have learned through socialization processes to find pleasure in fol-lowing the goals which their cultural system indicates and in experiencing unease when abandoning traditionally transmitted models. Mr Stevens, the butler in Kazuo Ishiguro's novel *The Remains of the Day* (1989), is obsessed by his search for "dignity". He desires ardently to know what it consists of and attempts to achieve it in his profession. He does not share the opinion of his colleague Mr Graham that dignity, like a woman's beauty, is a gift of nature, something that one has or does not have; he believes it is a conquest and that great efforts must be made to achieve it.

In order to gain dignity, models must be followed, and culture offers its repertoire of appropriate examples. Stevens found in his father his own personal model of dignity:

> If I try to describe to you what I believe made my father thus dis-tinguished, I may in this way convey my idea of what 'dignity' is. There was a certain story my father was fond of repeating over the years. I recall listening to him tell his visitors when I was a child, and then later, when I was starting out as a footman under his supervision. I remember him relating it again the first time I returned to see him after gaining my first post as a butler.
>
> (Ishiguro, 1989: 35)

This is a chain of cultural transmission. Stevens' father, his model, in turn follows a model of professionality which is derived from a story told to him and which he tells his son: that of a butler who followed his master to India and managed to maintain even in his new environment the high professional standard he had attained in England. Stevens says: "Clearly the story meant much to him. My father's generation was not one accustomed to discussing and analysing in the way ours is and I believe the telling and retelling of this story was as close as my father ever came to reflecting critically on the profession he practised" (Ishiguro, 1989: 36).

Stevens *père* particularly appreciated one episode in the story in which the model butler solved a delicate situation – a tiger under the dining-room table – with exceptional imperturbability, efficiency and discretion. Stevens *fils* believes that the story of the butler and the tiger inspired his father's professional life:

> When I look back over his career, I can see with hindsight that he must have striven throughout his years somehow to *become* that butler of his story. And in my view, at the peak of his career, my father achieved his ambition. For although I am sure he never had the chance to encounter a tiger beneath the dining table, when I think over all that I know or have heard concerning him, I can think of at least several instances of his displaying in abundance that very quality he so admired in the butler of the story.
>
> (Ishiguro, 1989: 37)

At the end of his day, Stevens thinks that, all in all, his whole life has been pure desolation. He has served his master to the best of his ability, as his models had taught him, but he now realizes that his devotion was wasted. The efforts of Lord Darlington to persuade His Majesty's Government to come to an agreement with the Nazis were the fatuous exercises of an amateur politician, even acts of shameful complicity. And yet, Stevens thinks, Lord Darlington could at least say that he had made his own errors, while he himself cannot even say that, because he had trusted his master. "What dignity is there in that?", he wonders, when he has come to the end of his search for that elusive quality.

A retired butler, whom Stevens meets by chance on the pier of the little town in which his hopes of starting a new life are shattered, consoles Stevens by reminding him of his original idea of dignity:

> What is the point in worrying oneself too much about what one could or could not have done to control the course one's life took? Surely it is enough that the likes of you and I at least *try* to make our small contribution count for something true and worthy. And if someone of us are prepared to sacrifice much in life in order to pursue such aspirations, surely that is in itself, whatever the outcome, cause for pride and contentment.
>
> (Ishiguro, 1989: 244)

Beyond success or failure in achieving our goals, we are encouraged by the culture in which we have grown up to be proud of having followed the models which were presented to us. But if our original culture has vanished in the meantime, what comfort is left to those at the end of their journey? They will no longer find one of themselves, one like themselves, who shares their world of values and speaks their language. We need adults and old people, because it is from them that cultural transmission starts, but, in order for that transmission to succeed, we need young people attentive to their history.

Chapter 9

The blind man's cane

WHERE DOES "I" BEGIN?

Our way of viewing people and their relationships with "external" reality reflects a new "ecological" sensitivity. We are now more aware than we were formerly of the fact that we must care for the environments in which people live, if we want to make sense of their actions. The science of psychology, which for much of its history has focused on the individual as a reality in its own right, now realizes the limitations of this approach and is beginning to explore the ways in which people and groups adapt dynamically to their environments.

We are now prepared to admit that intelligence does not only exist "inside" people's heads but is distributed between minds and things. If today I telephoned Anna to say "Happy Birthday!", it is only because this time, recalling the long face drawn when my absent-mindedness let me down in the past, I have plastered the house with notes saying "Remember Anna's birthday!" She was pleased to get my call, but is that because of my good memory or because of the little notes I left all around my bathroom? Both, I believe: in this case mind and environment worked hand in hand.

It was good teamwork: as I shaved, the note on the mirror reminded me to telephone. But it was my idea to stick it there in the first place, and also on the tube of toothpaste, the soap-dish and the fridge door. The invention of these little coloured notes – the modern equivalent of the knot in the hand-kerchief – certainly helped me a lot. Before I have had my morning coffee I do not really function at all, and after it I have to think of the morning's engagements; how could I have remembered that today is a unique event in Anna's life unless I had these little pieces of paper almost constantly before my eyes?

I remembered that today is Anna's birthday because the environment helped me. How do people manage without a diary, when they have to remember things like putting Laura's name down for the swimming course, passing by the town hall to pick up some papers, and going to the bank, in addition to normal living and working routines? We need help from the environment in order to sustain the operations our minds undertake. Norman (1992) and Zhang and Norman (1994) have shown that our way of framing problems is influenced by the way in which information is offered to us: different frames on my computer screen trigger different problem-solving strategies.

Intelligence is also distributed among people, because during our daily lives we generally live and work within groups. In a thoroughly integrated team, intelligence and responsibility are shared among various people and objects. Hutchins (1995) carried out an experiment on the navigation team of a US Navy aircraft carrier at San Diego, California. He showed how the ship's social and technological infrastructures operate as a single unit, in which what every person does depends on the actions of others and on how all the on-board equipment works. The navigation team collaborates with the piloting team and with the team actually commanding the ship, in turn linked with innumerable other groups which, in order to undertake their assigned tasks, all depend on a quantity of equipment ranging from radar and sonar to the turbines which supply energy to the entire ship.

Hutchins' study begins with a vivid description of the emergency which arose when the turbines suddenly broke down, leaving the enormous vessel out of control just as it was entering San Diego harbour, crowded with ferries, barges and sailing-boats. In this emergency, we see the sense-making processes analysed by Weick (1995) swing into action: control of the situation is regained thanks to the skills of the teams which make decisions in unexpected situations, improvising new forms of interaction among themselves and with the ship's equipment. This requires great coordination and flexibility – the two distinctive features of an efficient organization. We do not find ourselves faced with the isolated minds typical of the early cognitive studies, but with knowledge which is amply distributed among people and artifacts.

In his famous work *Steps to an Ecology of Mind* (1972), Gregory Bateson writes: "Suppose I am a blind man, and I use a stick. I go tap, tap, tap. Where do I start? Is my mental system bounded at the hand of the stick? Is it bounded to my skin? Does it start halfway up the stick? Does it start at the tip of the stick?" (Bateson, 1972: 459). The question is subtle: the stick, which is the channel carrying the information the blind man needs to walk along the street, is neither "outside" nor "inside" his cognitive system.

THE MEDIATION OF ARTIFACTS

The image of the blind man shows that it is difficult to draw a fine line between mind and external world. Clearly, the stick is not completely "inside" the blind man's mind; this is why his mind is not basically changed when he leans his stick against a chair in a café and sits down to enjoy an aperitif. What is far from clear for the dualistic mentality currently afflicting psychology is that the stick is not even completely "outside" the blind man's cognitive system either; it is an extension of his mind as he walks along. Of course, when he enters a restaurant, the privileged link between his mind and his stick is interrupted. If we are interested in eating, we must take into account things like cutlery, plates and glasses, which are now entering into a special relationship with our minds. "The ways in which mind is distributed depend crucially on the tools through which one interacts with the world, and these in turn depend on one's goals. The combination of goals, tools, and setting constitutes simultaneously the context of behavior and the ways in which cognition can be said to be distributed in that context" (Cole and Engeström, 1993: 13).

The blind man uses his stick to gain information about his surroundings. His mind carries out operations which depend in essential ways on the fact that he uses a stick, which filters available information and makes only certain experiences accessible. In one sense, we are all blind, and explore reality with the aid of instruments, artifacts, by means of which we come to know things and act in the world. Knowing and acting are not separate processes: I know Anna's state of mind the moment I phone her with my birthday greetings. My call not only tells me about Anna's present attitude, it also changes it – in my favour this time.

"External" realities become part of us when they act as tools helping us to achieve our goals. That intelligence also exists outside individual minds; this is an important acquisition for modern psychology because "Nothing has done more damage to sociocultural research on mental functioning than the doctrine that all things (including 'mind', 'culture' and the 'mental') must be either inside (the 'person') or outside (in the 'situation'), but not both. And not neither either" (Shweder, 1995: 17). Cultural psychology, inspired by Vygotsky, has developed a lively interest in artifacts as instruments of mediation (Cole, 1996).

What does mediation mean? What is an artifact? For example, without a computer, a table and a wall-socket providing me with electricity, I would not be able to write these pages, sitting in the Dolomites looking out at a circle of golden peaks. In order to write, I need a series of physical objects, including something as simple as a table. I also need other tools: knowledge of language, interest in the subject, and my recall of Bateson's text, which I can quote accurately because it is entrusted to the impersonal memory of a computer.

However, it was my mind which decided some time ago, before I left for the Dolomites, to choose this particular quotation and put it in a special file, and it was my sometimes rusty memory which brought to mind that quotation and told me to use it here. Like Anna's birthday greetings, when things go well, objects and mind work together gracefully as a team. Between the intention to write and the finished manuscript, there is a chain of activities –

imagining the aim and the issues of the discourse, seeking the most appropriate strings of words and typing them correctly – which are guided by artifacts in the same way as the blind man's walk is guided by his stick.

Artifacts are embodied plans. There are not two types of artifacts, physical and ideal, but only one type, as Mike Cole, of the University of California, San Diego, explains: "Cultural artifacts are simultaneously ideal (conceptual) and material. They are ideal in that they contain in coded form the interactions of which they were previously a part and which they mediate in the present. They are material in that they exist only insofar as they are embodied in material artifacts" (Note 4) (Cole, 1995a: 32).

HEDGEHOGS AND FLAMINGOES

Cultural psychologists like Cole, and Vygotsky before him, had very good reasons to think that artifacts control behaviour. But do they control it completely? This is not plausible, if we consider the human capacity to improvise using tools in unpredictable ways in everyday activities. In all American homes, the fridge door is the family's notice-board: no one planned it that way, but there is no more visible place to leave messages than on the smooth electric bosom of that universal nursemaid who cares for those of all ages, day in day out, throughout the United States.

Interaction with instruments, moreover, does not explain how plans which involve important investments in terms of time, energy and attention come into being and develop. Top-level goals which, once defined, activate numerous sub-goals over sometimes lengthy time-spans (unless such goals are changed in the meantime) do not necessarily emerge thanks simply to the presence of suitable artifacts. In general, it would seem to be reductive to view our world as a single gigantic artifact; we prefer to think of the world as a space to be explored with the help of the maps our culture offers us.

Mediation by artifacts tells us how to write a paper, pass an exam, or prepare supper for friends, but it does not tell us why we think these things worth doing. In order to answer this question, we must examine not artifacts *per se* but the social games which people, groups and organizations play through them. These games are strategic in character, i.e., they follow complex, sophisticated and often tortuous pathways in pursuit of goals which are not always declared or apparent at the start. Any instrument planned to interact with human actors is sucked into the vortex of the strategic games which enliven every social milieu. This is why human beings are incessantly obliged to innovate. They are really incapable of repeating an operation more than once in an identical fashion (Clancey, 1994, 1997), because each time the context – which includes their goals, opportunities present in the environment and the reactions of others – of their action changes. Since social games are highly creative, the effective uses of artifacts are equally unpredictable to a great extent: Ciborra (1996), in his study of the effects in different organizations of the use of Lotus Notes, a very popular cooperative software in the early 1990s, found that, in every peculiar context, the system performs functions unpredicted by its designers but, at the same time, does not perform some of the predicted ones.

Lewis Carroll (1865) gives us a delightfully witty image of what a social game really is in his description of the croquet game to which the Queen of Hearts invites Alice.

> 'Get to your places!' shouted the Queen in a voice of thunder, and people began running about in all directions, tumbling up against each other; however, they got settled down in a minute or two, and the game began. Alice thought she had never seen such a curious croquet-ground in all her life; it was all ridges and furrows; the balls were live hedgehogs, the mallets live flamingoes, and the soldiers had to double themselves up and to stand on their hands and feet, to make the arches. The chief difficulty Alice found was in managing her flamingo.
>
> (Carroll, 1865 [1994]: 87)

The fact that the flamingoes and hedgehogs, like human beings, could foresee the effects of their own and other people's actions and could also pursue their own goals makes them quite unforeseeable, as Alice quickly realizes:

> She succeeded in getting its body tucked away, comfortably enough, under her arm, with its legs hanging down, but generally, just as she had got its neck nicely straightened out, and was going to give the hedgehog a blow with its head, it would twist itself round and look up in her face, with such a puzzled expression that she could not help bursting out laughing: and as she got its head down, and was going to begin again, it was very provoking to find that the hedgehog had unrolled itself, and was in the act of crawling away ... Alice soon came to the conclusion that it was a very difficult game indeed.
>
> (Carroll, 1865 [1994]: 87–8)

Alice also discovers that the other players cheat outrageously, steal each other's hedgehogs, and have no honest idea of teamwork. The worst thing is that the Queen cannot bear to lose and so, for her adversaries, it is "Off with their heads!" Alarmed, Alice confides in the Cat.

> 'How do you like the Queen?' said the Cat in a low voice. 'Not at all,' said Alice: 'she's so extremely –' Just then she noticed that the Queen

was close behind her, listening: so she went on, ' – likely to win, that it's hardly worth while finishing the game.' The Queen smiled and passed on.

(Carroll, 1865 [1994]: 90)

Alice, wise child, has already realized that "honest dissimulation" as erudite treatises taught as long ago as the seventeenth century, is an essential ingredient of social games.

Carroll was able to imagine an utterly chaotic game because he set on his croquet-ground living, intelligent beings which, as such, are refractory towards any routine. Bateson (1972) rightly observes that, if Carroll had imagined a game without living beings – for example, with balls or clubs or doors – the players would have been faced with a task which could be carried out in a planned manner. Even if the ground had been irregular, the balls not round, and the clubs strangely shaped, the players would have been able to learn to use them and the game, although difficult, would not have been impossible. But when living beings, capable of following their own desires, are set down to play, the situation becomes highly unpredictable.

BOUNDARY LINES

Artifacts initially appear to control human activities, but when we examine them a little more closely, we see that in fact they do not. They do mediate between people and the environment, but this is because people, groups and organizations mediate between the artifacts and the environment which contains them: without an efficient network of social actors which design, use and look after them, we would not have properly functioning tools but only so much scrap iron, like the abandoned factories studied by industrial archaeology. It is human society in its various articulations which plays the role of a large framework of sense-making of the ambiguous situations of daily life.

Only recently has the word "culture" laid aside its colonial past, which entrusted it with the care of studying "other" distant worlds, "other" foreign societies.

Once upon a time, not so very long ago, when the West was a good deal more sure of itself, of what it was, and what it wasn't, the concept of culture had a firm design and a definite edge. At first, global and evolutionary, it simply marked the West, rational, historical, progressive, devotional, off from the Non-West, superstitious, static, archaic, magical. Later, when, for a host of reasons, ethical, political, and wistfully scientific, this seemed too crude, and too candid, the need for a more exact, more celebratory representation of the world elsewhere came into being, and the concepts shifted to the life-way-of-a-people form familiar to us now.

(Geertz, 1995: 42).

Now Western societies too have a culture, and know they have it. However, even in its revised and corrected version, the concept of culture remains ambiguous: we may think of it as something which embodies individuals and makes them act in a uniform way. This equivocation must be dismantled: "Culture" with a capital C is an empty category; what really exists is a more modest "culture" which coincides with the activity of people who use knowledge and acts in different real-life contexts (Wassmann, 1995). In this sense, culture is mainly made up of things done and not spoken, non-formalized and non-formalizable practices, and ways of acting of which we may not even be clearly aware.

Culture in everyday life is a little like Alice's croquet-ground, full of furrows and bumps:

> In contrast with the classic view, which posits culture as a self-contained whole made up of coherent patterns, culture can arguably be conceived as a more porous array of intersections where distinct processes criss-cross from within and beyond its borders. Such heterogeneous processes often derive from differences of age, gender, class, race, and sexual orientation.
>
> (Rosaldo, 1989: 103)

Our idea of culture is that it is not a closed space, but more like a system of boundaries. It is a way of taking seriously and appreciating differences among communities and heritages to the point of accepting the fact that measureless depths may separate them.

Thinking in terms of culture today means abandoning generalizations and accepting the essential specificity of social contexts (Mantovani, 1994). Culture is a boundary which we cross every time we find ourselves faced with "another" whose differences we perceive and respect. Bakhtin (1981) promoted this idea of culture as a meeting-place:

> One must not, however, imagine the realm of culture as some sort of spatial whole, having boundaries but also having internal territory. The realm of culture has no internal territory: it is entirely distributed along the boundaries, boundaries pass everywhere, through its every aspect. Every cultural act lives essentially on the boundaries: in this is its seriousness and significance. Abstracted from boundaries it loses its soil, it becomes empty, arrogant, it degenerates and dies."
>
> (Bakhtin, 1981)

A boundary along which exchanges take place (Notes 5 and 6): this is our non-monolithic view of culture. A system of majestic rivers and tributaries which cross and nourish a vast territory; rivers spanned by bridges, ferries and boats which make of them not barriers but passable frontiers between intercommunicating areas. Travellers from far countries awaiting their ferry on the river bank can meet, to exchange objects and stories unknown in their own countries.

Part IV

Culture in education

In her adventures on the other side of the looking-glass, Alice meets the Red Queen, who seizes her by the hand and drags her along in a mad rush. "Faster! Faster!" she shrieks. Alice runs as fast as she can, the wind whistling in her ears, her feet skimming the ground. She notices that the surrounding countryside remains stationary. "Faster!" exhorts the Queen. Alice is about to collapse in exhaustion when suddenly they both stop, and Alice realizes that they are still under the same tree they were at the beginning. The Queen demands to know why this should seem strange to Alice.

> 'Well, in *our* country,' said Alice, still panting a little, 'you'd generally get to somewhere else – if you ran very fast for a long time, as we've been doing.' 'A slow sort of country!' said the Queen. 'Now, *here*, you see, it takes all the running *you* can do, to keep in the same place. If you want to get somewhere else, you must run at least twice as fast as that!' 'I'd rather not try, please!' said Alice. 'I'm quite content to stay here.'
>
> (Carroll, 1872 [1984]: 42)

The whimsical grace of Carroll's tale suggests reflection: however fast we run, we carry with us the web of our culture and, on our arrival, like Alice, we find ourselves where we started.

Chapter 10, *Cultivating memory*, shows how each of us enters at birth upon a conversation which began before we arrived. In order to take part in it, each of us has to know what happened before – we must know our history, which contains lights and shadows. Remembering is our first step into the future. We do not in fact move towards the future. The future moves towards us, enters us. The new generations, to which each society transmits its values, are one of the faces of the future.

Chapter 11, *The sheriff comes for Virgil*, uses some real-life American episodes to consider the two approaches which currently dominate educational environments: one which views education as a process of cultural transmission, and the other which gives top priority to transmission of information, enhanced by the new computer technologies. Technologists and the mass media seem to believe that, in the near future, the new information technologies will improve the living conditions of people and organizations, thanks to the greater amount of information available.

Chapter 12, *Crossing borders*, rejects the technological approach and stresses the dangers of information overload. The "saturated self", swamped with messages, is set opposite to the transcultural self which combines the elements of two cultures, having acquired new cultural codes without losing the previous ones. The challenge of the future does not lie in the mass of information which we will able to process, but in our capacity to offer students, parents and teachers the appropriate spaces and the necessary tools for critical elaboration of transmitted memories, for personal recognition of cultural differences, and for nurturing respect of others' identities and values.

Chapter 10

Cultivating memory

AN ENDLESS CONVERSATION

The fearless concubines of the rajah of Bali and the Dane Helms, speechless in the face of their silent dive into death, the *nahua* "sun counters" and the Spanish missionaries who invited them to a theological discussion on the smoking ruins of Tenochtitlàn, the headhunter Ilingot Tukbaw and his American "brother" Renato Rosaldo, who refused to fight in Vietnam – all these people encountered one another on boundaries between different worlds. For some of them, like Alvar Nuñez Cabeza de Vaca confronted with the New World, the meeting marked the onset of an upheaval, personal and intimate, but nevertheless overwhelming. For others, like "Christoferens" Columbus and Hernàn Cortez, it was the first step along a path leading to the destruction of the other.

People who meet one another have to overcome enormous distances in their visions of life, death, war, hope and happiness. Let us imagine a crowded tavern in a frontier post, full of travellers from all parts of the world. The room is a Babel of languages. Smoke from the kitchen, the smell of men, animals and food, outbursts of laughter or rage all form the background to an animated conversation composed of a mix of business deals, cheerful songs, dirty jokes and confidences between friends. Every so often voices are lowered to pass on a titbit of gossip or a piece of dangerous information, but otherwise the din is considerable.

Groups of people sit down at the tables and begin to eat and drink together, or one person gets up and goes across the room to greet an old friend or meet a new one. Differences are as important as, or even more important than, affinities in the conversation: who, during a party, would want to spend the entire evening with a person they already know well, who is not telling them anything particularly new? (Well, in the case of Anna, it would be different: I know her very well and I never get tired of being in her company, but this is because she is the most unusual person I know. Often, when I see her lost in thought, I wonder what she is hatching up behind that impenetrable and obstinate little countenance).

Sometimes the interlocutors have different opinions; then the conversation becomes a discussion, more or less friendly or argumentative. Kenneth Burke (1957), explaining the function of language, imagined a scene illuminating the function of the cultural framework in which individuals enter from the very beginnings of their social lives:

> Imagine that you enter a parlor. You come late. When you arrive, others have long preceded you, and they are engaged in a heated discussion, a discussion too heated for them to pause and tell you exactly what it is about. In fact, the discussion had already begun before any of them got there, so that no one present is qualified to retrace for you all the steps that had gone on before.
>
> (Burke, 1957: 95–6)

Burke's example highlights an essential feature of the relationship between individual and culture: we always start from something that already exists, that has already been going on for some time, about which we know very little. Since our birth, we find ourselves immersed in a social environment which was already there before we arrived. We cannot choose our mother, father, birthplace or mother tongue; we may learn to know them better, but we are always obliged to use the maps that are passed on to us by our predecessors. Like Alice, we are not very far from our starting point even if we start running furiously. However daring our explorations of reality, we cannot eliminate this *a priori* element. We are allowed to take part in the discussion, but not to begin it. We can only enter it at a certain moment and hope that what we have to say will interest someone.

We cannot grasp its overall sense. The others, even if they wished, cannot help us. Everyone who was in the room when we arrived is in the same situation: they arrived late too. We do not know how the conversation arose, nor even if it had a beginning. There are no reliable reports. Every culture aims at revealing to its members how things originally started: "In the beginning, God created the heaven and the earth. And the earth was without form and void; and darkness was upon the face of the deep. And the Spirit of God moved upon the face of the waters" (Genesis, I, 1–2). This is the story that is told in many communities, but other communities have other, different stories – a fact which we cannot and should not ignore. Do we even know if we are all talking about the same thing, perhaps using different words? Or is Burke's parlour just another name for the Tower of Babel, where everyone kept talking in a language inaccessible to others?

So what can we do? Why, what everyone else does, says Burke:

> You listen for a while until you decide that you have caught the tenor of the argument; then you put in your oar. Someone answers; you answer

him; another comes to your defence; another aligns himself against you, to either the embarrassment or gratification of your opponent, depending on the quality of your ally's assistance. However, the discussion is interminable. The hour grows late, you must depart. And you do depart, with the conversation still in progress.

(Burke, 1957: 95–6)

The end of the conversation, like its beginning, is also beyond our range. Like Stevens the butler at the end of his search for "dignity", we may feel the need to understand the sense of our personal contribution to the conversation, but the fact remains that when we have to leave the room the discussion flows on, like an unexhausted river, lapping a thousand banks and a thousand new arguments.

AUNT ITKA'S BANDAGE

Although beginning and end escape us, we can glean illuminating scraps of information of the conversation we enter. Previous narrations, like that of Columbus's "taking possession" of the New World, reveal how things have gone, not at the beginning of time but in a recent phase of that heated debate, animated conversation, or serene exchange of thoughts which mark the history of relations among human societies. Recalling centuries-old episodes may help us to understand the present more than those chronicles (of politics or sports) which suffocate our minds every time we turn on the TV.

As history unfolds a little of itself to us, we may glimpse something which clarifies what is happening. For those who, like us, are immersed in the technological din polluting every corner of our crowded tavern, memory and attention – ours and everyone's – are the most precious of resources. Memories are inextricably entwined, because we can understand ourselves only through our relationships with others. As each of us is "constructed" by the glances of those surrounding us, so the history of our society is illuminated by that of societies with which it came into contact. We have seen, for example, how the various moments of the conquest of the New World reveal traits of the Old.

Attention to history requires us to reserve space for silence and reflection, to allow memories to surface and to be contemplated. Memory needs time to consider situations, persons and affects, and to explore their reasons, results and meanings. Memory ruminates on a moral problem – it deals with the third function of culture, the identification of values. Memory harks back to the signs left by those who have been crushed. Their fate requires an explanation on the moral plane, since it is they who ask "Why?" Sitting in our crowded corner of the frontier tavern – which we can now imagine as a café in an international airport, packed with self-important businessmen attached to cell-phones and vociferous, avid tourists – we can no longer hear the still, small voice of the great tragedies of our century.

We must listen carefully if we want to hear it, because silence, reserve and even shame are the characteristics of victims. Victims do not want to ruin the party or attract too much attention to themselves. The narrator of *See: Under 'Love'* by David Grossman (1986) has an aunt, Itka, who survived a Nazi extermination camp in which her prison number was tattooed on her forearm.

> When I married Ruth, Aunt Itka came to the wedding with a bandage on her arm, 'to hide the number tattooed on it' because she did not want to spoil the cheerful atmosphere of the party. But me, my heart was filled to bursting with the pity I felt for her. . . . For the whole evening, I couldn't take my eyes off her arm. I felt as if, under that clean bandage, Aunt Itka hid a bottomless abyss which sucked everything and everyone into it, the festive room, the guests, the happiness.
>
> (Grossman, 1986: 140)

Aunt Itka's bandage overlaps the serene metaphor of the conversation which was our starting point and destroys it. Burke's parlour full of kind, happy people vanishes, to be replaced by a sequel of horrors which the bandage vainly tries to cancel, to silence, to hide by pretending to cover the open wound in our conscience. The victims, all victims, are ashamed of what happened. They suffer not only because of the memory of their torment and loss, but also because they can no longer live in a world which appears destitute of any moral justification. They cannot forget what human beings are capable of. A boot crushing a human face, Orwell's *1984* image which sums up the horror of an inhuman regime, has had such success during this century that it still has ardent, even brazen, supporters.

We have no reason to believe that this century, or this millennium, will be morally any better, unless we improve – but how? In Grossman's view, it is not enough to be informed, instructed, intelligent. Some Nazis were all of these things. Grossman describes a conversation between the death camp commander, Neigel, and an old Jewish prisoner, Wasserman. Wasserman believes that it is their capacity to choose which makes human beings human, and Neigel tells him that he, a Nazi, has chosen to obey his party: "I have made a choice too! The choice to put into practice the values of the Movement and the Party, and their orders to kill. Am I less of a man than you for that reason? If a man is capable of doing something, that means it's human, doesn't it?" (Grossman, 1986: 97).

Wasserman does not agree; killing is not a true choice, because choosing means affirming humanity's highest values. Again Neigel insists:

'And I have chosen the alternative. I have chosen to kill. I *decided* it. How can you say that this is not a choice? Do you know how much effort was required to do such a thing?' Wasserman replies: 'One does not begin to kill, Herr Neigel. One only continues to do so. And the same goes for beginning to hate one's neighbour or hunting him. One only continues. But one must choose, consciously, not to kill, not to hate, and this is the root of diversity'.

(Grossman, 1986: 97)

UNPRECEDENTED REPENTANCE

Wasserman's question is indeed of formidable dimensions: how can we change? How can we stop hurting and destroying others? How can we avoid repeating old mistakes? We noted Columbus's decision, when he took the first step on the path which led to the annihilation of the native population. Who can truly say it was wrong? At that time, few Europeans doubted that the conquest of the New World was a magnificent feat, albeit a little brutal. Some more tender-hearted missionaries like Bartolomè de las Casas pointed this out to constituted authority, denouncing the damage done to the Indios, the Spaniards' unbounded greed for gold, and their cruelty towards women and children, who were raped, tortured and given to war dogs to eat (Todorov, 1982). The idea behind the monks' protest was that, as many Spaniards were not behaving like good Christians, it would be a good thing to restrict their excesses. Nothing more.

No European really thought it might be acceptable to leave the Aztecs' souls in the Devil's hands, there was no doubt about that. What doubts could anyone have, faced with the revolting spectacle meeting the Spaniards' eyes in the temples of Tenochtitlàn, littered with statues daubed with the blood of human victims? Cortez reported to the Emperor Carlos V that he had forbidden human sacrifices, respecting the Christian religion and the laws in force in Spain: no one would have reproved him for such a decision. In this case, as in that of *suttee*, there was an unmeasurable distance between cultures: what was divine for one was devilish for the other.

Cortez's second letter to Carlos V, written on 3 October 1520 from Segura de la Frontera in New Spain, reveals the cultural shock suffered by the *conquistadores* when faced with the Aztec religion:

The statues of the idols worshipped by these people are much larger than a tall man. They are made of a mixture of the vegetables and seeds which they eat. These they grind up and mix with the blood of human hearts which they tear from the open breasts of men still living. With the blood gouting from these hearts, they make a paste with the mashed seeds until they have a quantity sufficient to model such large statues.

Once they have fashioned them, they sacrifice to them new human
hearts and paint the faces of the idols with the blood.

(Cortez, 1520 [1963]: 112–13)

Cortez reacted promptly to what he saw on entering the "great mosque"
of Tenochtitlàn:

I had the largest idols toppled from their pedestals and ordered them to
be thrown down the steps. Then I had the chapels cleaned of the blood
of human sacrifice and, in place of the idols, I caused to be raised the
image of Our Lady and other saints, arousing the indignation of Montezuma and his people. They begged me not to do it, saying that if the rest
of the population knew about it, they would rise against me, since they
were convinced that those idols were the source of all their temporal
wealth.

(Cortez, 1520 [1963]: 112–13)

We may consider Cortez's decision quite intolerant, the more so if we
consider that the Aztec ruler Montezuma said that his people's traditional
religious practices might be contaminated in the course of time with errors
and stated that he was prepared to follow the recommendations of Cortez,
who had only just arrived from the land of the gods and who might therefore
be better informed about the matter.

Yet, if some bizarre time machine were to set us down, now, in Cortez's
shoes, what would we do? Collect anthropological evidence of Aztec
sacrificial rites, or try to halt the slaughter? Take time off to write a fine
scientific report, or set to work cleaning blood-encrusted statues and stair-
cases? Study the order of precedence of the dignitaries in claiming the various parts of the bodies of the sacrificial victims reserved as food for the
nahua aristocracy, or turn aside revolted from the scenes at the foot of the
temple steps? Encounters with radically different cultures, although they
may enhance our comprehension of human diversity, as Geertz points out,
also increase our confusion: there are experiences which we really cannot
catch in our nets.

The problem does lie within our cultural grid. Western culture has
developed a peculiar characteristic which Bernard Lewis (1995) clearly
highlights:

In setting out to conquer, subjugate, and despoil other peoples, the
Europeans were merely following the example set them by their neigh-
bors and predecessors and, indeed, conforming to the common practice
of mankind ... The interesting questions are not why they tried, but
why they succeeded and why, having succeeded, they repented of their

success as of a sin. The success was unique in modern times; the repent-
ance, in all of recorded history.

(Lewis, 1995: 73)

It is true that, since the times of Cain and Abel, the history of human
societies has been an unwearying tale of ferocity, stupidity and violence (but,
to be honest, not just of them) but we have to admit that inside Western
societies, together with brazen manifestations of cynicism, we do see the
emergence of moral requirements which are more sophisticated than in the
past. We can now find ears attuned to the sorrow of Pablo Neruda (1950),
the poet of Latin-American identity and 1971 Nobel prize-winner for literature, who evoked the appearance of the Spanish in the Caribbean with these
words

> Sparrow-hawks devastated the islands.
> Guanahanì was the first
> in this history of martyrs.
> The children of the clay saw
> their smiles dashed from their faces,
> their fragile deer-like figures struck,
> and in death too they did not understand.
> They were chained and wounded,
> they were burned and scorched,
> they were covered with bites, and buried.
> And when time had finished its waltz among the palm-trees,
> the green hall was emptied.

(Neruda, 1950: 148)

The sense of past events is changing. Fathers' successes become defeats for
their children. The elimination of the other is experienced as an amputation
of oneself. The model is now Alvar Nuñez, who was a shaman among the
Indios and walked with them for seven years, from the Atlantic to the
Pacific, after leaving San Lucar de Barrameda to conquer his little piece of
the New World. He became half-Spanish, half-Indio, and was suspected of
being a traitor and an apostate. He was in fact a link between two worlds, a
product of that hybridization which contact between cultures continually
creates.

Western culture is critically re-examining its history and redefining its
values, in an attempt to fix higher ethical standards for itself. Lewis observes
that

> *imperialism, sexism* and *racism* are words of Western coinage, not
> because the West invented these evils, which are alas universal, but
> because the West recognized and named and condemned them as evils

and struggled mightily – and not entirely in vain – to weaken their hold
and to help their victims. If, to borrow a phrase, Western culture does
indeed 'go', *imperialism, sexism* and *racism* will not go with it. More
likely casualties will be the freedom to denounce them and the effort to
end them.

(Lewis, 1995: 79)

SO MANY EXCUSES FOR GUERNICA

It must be admitted that the gap between the principles and effective practices of modern Western societies widens daily and, with it, our confusion.
While the media continually spew out reports of acts of aggression towards
children, women and immigrants, the idea that resorting to violence is
always unacceptable is gaining ground. While the entire natural environment of our planet is under attack, mass awareness of the importance of
ecology is spreading. Like strange flowers, new values grow on the trunk of
Western societies and we cannot get rid of them simply by considering them
as manifestations of false conscience: we have seen, *à propos* of the hunting
rituals of Pigmies and Eskimos, that principles are important even when they
are not observed.

Principles mark the distance between what is done in everyday life and
what should be done in an ideal world. When the gap between the daily
practices and moral principles of a society begins to be really disturbing,
people try to reduce the hiatus by taking a few steps in the right direction.
The first step consists of remembering, of going back to focus on their history, although this may be difficult because it brings to light blame and
shame. Every society has its own memories of glory and horror, generosity
and greed, courage and cowardice. Understanding tradition means seeing its
limitations and crimes and recognizing them as such.

Sometimes recognition is made. One example: on 26 April 1937, aircraft
of the Condor Legion, sent by Hitler to support Franco's forces during the
Spanish Civil War, carried out a ferocious attack on Guernica, the holy city
of the Basque country. It was the first bombing mission in history directed
against a civilian population. Three-quarters of the buildings in the town
were razed to the ground, more than one thousand people were killed and a
similar number seriously injured. One of the aims of this attack, as well as to
sow terror among the population, was to conduct an experiment, anticipat-
ing more systematic aggressive operations in the future. The experiment was
a success.

Guernica was the visiting-card with which the Nazi regime presented itself
on the world scene. Picasso caught the sense of the event and entrusted it to
his celebrated, gigantic, tragic painting. The Condor Legion was triumph-
antly welcomed back in Berlin, with decorations, awards and promotion for

all the valiant officers. Later, during the Second World War, several British cities – of which Coventry is the prime example – suffered carpet bombing designed to reduce them to heaps of smoking rubble and to break civilian morale. When the pendulum of war swung the other way, numerous German cities – including that Baroque gem, Dresden – were obliged to drink from the same bitter chalice which the Luftwaffe had offered Guernica, Coventry and many others.

Exactly sixty years later, on 26 April 1997, the German parliament unanimously expressed its regret for what the Condor Legion had done at Guernica, and asked the German president, Herzog, to present the apologies of the nation to the people of Guernica. The parliament and the president of a powerful state, which might legitimately have claimed no direct bond with the Nazi regime, confessed "blame". Perhaps this gesture did not count for very much for the victims, but it was a positive sign. Apologies will not bring people back to life, and making excuses and refunding damage cannot compensate for human suffering. But to ask for pardon is necessary if we wish to retain some mark of self-respect.

However, granting pardon is difficult to imagine. Who has the right to grant it? Not the victims, considering that, in them, all humanity has been wounded. Who can condone the Holocaust? Or the Soviet gulags and their icy marshes into which entire nations were swallowed for decades? Or the other massacres, of the Armenians or the Cambodians, far from the limelight, to the total indifference of the media, ready to mobilize only at the prospect of events guaranteeing high viewing figures interrupted every five minutes by consumer advertising? These days, human suffering occupies prime TV time in the early evening, as all of us know from views of film stars arriving, surrounded by clouds of photographers and video-cameras, in the refugee camps of Central Africa, showing us how children die of hunger and dehydration.

Italy too was present in the sky above Guernica, in the shape of several three-engined Savoia-Marchetti aircraft flanking the glorious Condor Legion for the occasion, but there is no indication that the Italian government presented excuses of any kind. The fact is that very few Italians worry about these aspects of their history, and their parliament cannot find time to discuss such minutiae. It's all in the past, to be forgotten: no memory, no reflection, no guilt, no excuses. Has the Italian government presented its excuses, for instance, to Ethiopia, for the massacres ordered there by General Graziani, Viceroy of Italian East Africa, in response to the attack made on him at Addis Ababa on 19 February 1937?

To give an idea of the kind of reprisals involved, we can recall just one episode, buried together with a thousand others in the convenient national amnesia: the attack on the holy city of Debrà Libanòs, ceremonial heart of the Ethiopian Coptic Church, representing Christianity by ancient tradition. In the course of their 150-kilometre march from Addis Ababa, General

Maletti's troops burned 115,422 *tukuls* (huts), three churches and one convent, incidentally killing 2,523 "rebels" on the way. On 18 May, Debrà Libanòs was surrounded and, between 19 and 26 May 1937, one month after Guernica, 1,600 monks, elderly priests, young deacons and simple pilgrims were executed. The 5,500 members of the religious community who were not killed on the spot were deported to the concentration camp of Danane, in Somaliland, where more than half died of disease and hardship. The conditions in which they were kept may, unfortunately, be imagined.

"A Roman example of prompt, inflexible rigour", commented General Graziani, in the laconic style that the fascist regime considered apt for such glorious accomplishments. Historians Ian Campbell, of the University of Nairobi, and Degife Gabre Tsadik, of the University of Addis Ababa, referred to the affair in autumn 1997 in *Studi Piacentini*, a review founded by the historian Angelo Del Boca, of the University of Turin. It does not appear that the Italian parliament, government or head of state profited by the sixtieth anniversary of the Debrà Libanòs massacre to present any kind of apology.

French anthropologist Dan Sperber wrote:

> One scene left its mark on my infancy: my father used to sit in an armchair in the sitting-room, absolutely motionless, with his hands clasped together, staring into space. My mother would whisper: 'Don't disturb your father, he's working'. I was perplexed. Later, I too became an intellectual and went to Ethiopia as an ethnographer. There, I heard a Dorze mother whisper to her child: 'Don't disturb your father, he's nourishing his ancestors'. So I sat on top of the hill from which you can see the Dorze market-place, and stayed there motionless, staring into space.
>
> (Sperber, 1974: 143–4)

What we call "thinking", "pondering", or "trying to understand what is happening", people of traditional cultures call "nourishing ancestors", appealing to memory, remaining in contact with roots. They know that our frantic rushing about has a starting point which supports and contains it. If we want to understand where we are going, to imagine the future, we must first know where we came from: this is why we must face our tradition in a serious and critical manner. It opens up the future to us only if we can free ourselves from the errors which produced horrible crimes in the past and which we must recognize and detest.

In Europe, the United States, and indeed throughout the world, we can see the collapse of the ideal of integration that many people consider a paternalistic project aiming at cancelling cultural differences. The dialogue takes place not "in spite of" but "thanks to" those differences. Tolerance is no longer enough; on the contrary, sometimes it merely seems to complicate things. Must the Italians tolerate the Ethiopians, or must the Ethiopians, who have suffered great wrongs, be asked to tolerate the Italians? Who must tolerate something like the Debrà Libanòs massacre?

In the United States, where encounters and confrontations between different cultures are an essential ingredient of the country's history, must the whites tolerate the Sioux, or must the few remaining Sioux tolerate the *wasichu*, the Sioux word for the whites, "those who steal fat, and are never content"? And what about the Africans, dragged in chains to the New World, and the other religious or national groups who founded, with immense sufferings, new homes on the other side of the Atlantic? Who must tolerate whom? Tolerance is not enough. Understanding difference, appreciating it, is the new frontier of our increasingly variegated global world.

Chapter 11

The sheriff comes for Virgil

PUMPKINS AND TEDDY-BEARS

Arrested in the classroom, by the sheriff. Handcuffed with his hands behind his back, before his stupefied classmates, and removed to the police station. A drug pedlar, paedophile, kidnapper? Nothing of the kind. The criminal was Virgil, aged five, accused of causing bodily harm and arrested. At the police station, he was asked to sign the report confirming his arrest, and Virgil, proud of being able to do things like a grown-up, signed. "I did it all on my own", he later told reporters, "I signed the report with my name, and added my home address." Quite a feat for a five-year-old.

This episode occurred on 28 October 1996 in a small town about 20 miles from New Orleans, Louisiana. Virgil had thrown a pumpkin at a classmate. The pumpkin was in the schoolroom because the children were making decorations for Halloween, scooping out pumpkins and cutting slits in them for eyes and mouth. Then, as we all know, they put them over their heads and sally forth in the evening to pester their neighbours for "trick or treat". The police had been called in by the headmistress, who insisted that Virgil should be handcuffed in class, as an example to his companions. An example of what? Clearly, of what happens when someone has not got the slightest idea of what education means.

Protests and fierce debates followed. The PTA representative declared to the press that it was a crying shame that adult, professional teachers, presumed to be expert at their jobs, felt obliged to call in the police to deal with an over-excited five-year-old. The point here is not whether Virgil was a hyperactive little pest or not, but rather: how had things reached such a pass that the only way of dealing with the child was considered to be to call the police and have him hauled off to jail in irons? Virgil's mother, Deanna, admitted that her son was difficult to manage, but she was dissatisfied with the fact that the school authorities handled the problem simply by sending the boy out of class. Often, an hour after he had left for school, he was back home. "What kind of education is that?" Deanna asked. Yes indeed, what does education mean?

Another example of handcuffs in American schools occurred on 22 April 1997, when a little girl of six from Largo, Florida, made headlines in the *Tampa Tribune* and thereafter throughout the national press. The child had stood in front of a television screen, thereby hindering her classmates from watching a video on crime prevention which the police were presenting to the class. Exactly what it was that had upset the child, the images on the screen or the presence of the police, is unknown. The fact remains that she refused to move and reacted to attempts to move her forcibly by screaming furiously, kicking and spitting at a policeman and the headmaster. Resisting arrest is a serious crime in the United States. And as for spitting at headmasters, well, that's just unthinkable, anywhere around the globe. American law does not foresee arrest for minors aged under seven, who are not considered capable of committing a crime, but behaviour like this definitely required handcuffs.

One detail: before starting to scream, the little girl threw her teddy-bear at the policeman. A pathetic gesture of defiance made by a child of six – separating herself from her transitional object and sending it as a messenger towards the strange, terrifying adult world – which was not understood by those present. A teddy may be softer than Virgil's pumpkin, but its effect as regards handcuffing was identical. After her arrest, the little girl was taken to a detention centre for minors, where she remained for several hours before her father arrived to collect her. Her grandmother, who had offered to fetch her from the school, was told that the child could not be handed over to her granny because she was in a state of arrest. The little rebel was suspended from school for bad conduct and, on her return, was assigned to a special class.

Episodes like this lead us to believe that, in some parts of the affluent Western world, educating children is becoming too difficult, perhaps impossible, certainly too much for institutions such as schools. Passing the buck to the sheriff is easier. The message is: "Virgil, behave yourself and don't go around throwing pumpkins at people, or you'll end up in jail, get that? And the same goes for you, you wicked little slinger of teddy-bears."

JONATHAN THE SEX FIEND

You simply can't trust children, you can never relax your vigilance. Even model children – blond, blue-eyed, bespectacled and well-behaved – can become precocious criminals as soon as you take your eye off them. On 24 September 1996, Jonathan, aged six, in his first year of school at Lexington, North Carolina, kissed a classmate (who had *asked* him to) on the cheek. Caught in the act, Jonathan was punished with a "disciplinary report" according to the School Conduct Code, given out to all parents at the beginning of the school year, and was forbidden to attend an ice-cream party for students with perfect attendance.

What was so terribly perverse about Jonathan's kiss? Jane Martin, spokeswoman for the Lexington school authorities, pointed out that the code expressly forbade kissing among school companions. Kissing was, without exception, a form of *sexual harassment*. "She gave me the sexual harassment policy", said Jonathan's mother to a reporter from *The New York Times*, "and proceeded to tell Jonathan that if he was caught again kissing, hugging, or hand-holding, he would be suspended." Jonathan's punishment unleashed a debate throughout America. "At this rate," said Jonathan's mother in fury, "they'll stop children even holding hands." But Ms Martin did not budge from her position: "If you expect students in junior high and high school to understand why unwanted sexual advances are wrong, then you have to start by teaching respect for others when they're young." It appears that kissing is, in Ms Martin's mind, simply to be wanting in respect.

These are not isolated cases. The new law of the State of California on sexual harassment, which authorizes school heads to suspend children only from the fourth grade onwards, was criticized on the ground that children under ten cannot be punished for sexual harassment. For these "educators" Jonathan was nothing less than a potential rapist. The words of someone like Ms Martin, representing school policy, sound appalling to discerning people. "How can we apply adult sexual norms to children barely old enough to control their bladders?", the *Boston Globe* asked its perplexed readers. If educators are unable to appreciate the difference between Jonathan's chaste little kiss and a rape, how can six-year-olds appreciate it? And if educators are neither interested in nor capable of appreciating the meaning of human actions, what kind of educators are they? They are simply crude cops trying to control children's behaviour to fit their particular, crude vision of society.

The frequent presence of police in school environments revealed by these stories shows how the meaning of "education" is changing for the worse. In Bruner's (1996) view, education has the task of assisting people in their "meaning-making" activities, i.e., in their attempts at constructing a sensible physical and social world. In order to do this, people have to interpret their own experiences, discriminating between various contexts and situations and assessing the adequacy of actions to social values and norms. "Meaning making involves situating encounters with the world in their appropriate cultural contexts in order to know 'what they are about'" (Bruner, 1996: 3). Education means setting Jonathan's kiss in its social and moral context: what was Jonathan really doing when he accepted his little friend's polite request to be kissed on the cheek?

The context is precisely what his School Conduct Code chose to ignore. Why, we might ask, does it neglect the difference between a little kid of six and an adolescent of sixteen, between Jonathan's kiss and an aggressive and violent action? Above all, why does it not take into account the fact that Jonathan's little companion had *asked* him to kiss her? The Code purposely excludes such minutiae. It serves to establish rules to be applied automatically and indiscriminately, thus avoiding debates, discussions and above all discernment. Why should education teach kids how to tell the difference between a friendly kiss and an attempt at rape?

Should we laugh or cry at such stories? We cannot just put them aside as not worthy of our attention: they tell us that the actor's goals and the characteristics of the situation do not interest anyone among professionals of education. We see the triumph of an educational perspective taken to extremes: follow the letter of the law, forget the spirit. The third function of culture which we identified in Chapter 8, *Pride and dignity*, examines the matter of principles and of their relevance to the moral careers of individuals in a manner far removed from the way of thinking of Jane Martin and her Code. The Code seems to require individuals simply to conform to social norms and established rules, whereas principles have a wider and deeper orientative value.

PRINCIPLES IN EDUCATION

Principles do not encode current practices – on the contrary, they often contradict them. Principles are products not of consensus but of tradition, which imposes them on members of the community. These characteristics are clearly highlighted in the work of Jonathan Smith (1982) on the hunting rituals of several different cultures, ranging from Eskimos pursuing polar bears in Siberia to pigmy bands hunting elephant in Central and Southern Africa. Everywhere, prescriptions on how hunting must be carried out if the meat of the slain animal is to be legitimate food for the tribe are highly restrictive. The rituals regularly lay down quite impracticable actions, for example, that the animal may be attacked only while it faces the hunters head-on or while it is running towards them, that it may only be struck in certain parts of its body, or that the hunters, before killing it, must praise it for its grace and strength and apologize for the act they are about to carry out.

In human groups depending on hunting for their survival, these complex rituals cannot often be scrupulously respected in daily life. Neither Eskimos nor Pigmies can afford the luxury of hunting according to established ritual, nor can they afford to be too fastidious in refusing food from animals killed in a forbidden manner. Then why are impracticable rules established? What meaning can they have, if they seem to be designed just to be broken? If we believe that rules reflect the actual behaviour of the members of a given community, we expect that those members will respect them scrupulously in their daily practices. Yet the opposite occurs: rules often contradict everyday practices. Smith's explanation is that ritual deliberately aims at detaching the everyday world from the ideal one.

What people do in everyday reality, in confused and often dangerous situations, rarely fits what they think should be done. Ritual makes manifest the discrepancy existing between the two worlds, daily and ideal: "It provides the means for demonstrating that we know what ought to have been done, what ought to have taken place. It provides an occasion for reflection and rationalization of the fact that what ought to have been done was not done, what ought to have taken place did not occur" (Smith, 1982: 63). In the hurly-burly of daily existence, ritual allows us to preserve at least the idea of how things should be done in a perfectly ordered world: "Ritual represents the creation of a controlled environment where the variables of ordinary life may be displaced precisely because they are felt to be so overwhelmingly present and powerful. Ritual is a means of performing the way things ought to be in conscious tension to the way things are, in such a way that their ritualized perfection is recollected in the ordinary, uncontrolled course of things" (Smith, 1982: 63).

Ritual is a criticism of situations, not a reflection of them: people can (and in a certain sense must) be dissatisfied with what they do, even if their actions conform to the requirements of their environment. The hunter knows very well that, if he really wants to kill his bear, he cannot go up to the animal and explain that he respects and venerates him like an ancestor before killing him. But he also knows – ritual requires him to confirm it publicly – that killing cannot be done with impunity, that the bear is part of the sacred order of things, and that without that order life would be bereft of part of its sense. The contradiction between ritual and everyday life confers tension upon everyday experience, which is extended between the two poles of what people think ought to be done and what is actually done. A bad conscience, ritual suggests, is better than no conscience at all. This is far from the simple problem of obeying or not obeying a School Conduct Code.

When professionals in education reduce moral problems simply to respecting rules, they seem to lose sight of the most serious dimension of principles, which is to establish goals intrinsically worthy of respect. Such "educators" can no longer speak of moral values and they have to be content with laying down rules and punishing those who do not obey them. Education as a moral process vanishes, to give way to the capture and processing of information by isolated individuals. Meanings are uncertain and controversial: they must thus be outlawed from school and left to individual conscience, if there is anyone who can afford the luxury of having one. School does not concern itself with the matter; it's up to the family. This is why the Lexington school authorities were not interested in knowing *why* their little girl should wish to hurl her teddy-bear at the policeman. The school has its Code, the families have been informed about it, and that's that.

THE INFORMATION MODEL

Until the beginning of the modern age, many trades, arts and professions were taught by often powerful guilds, in which the training of "apprentices" under expert "masters" was only one aspect of a more extensive network of solidarity. The guilds planned the development of many kinds of activity, negotiated taxes with local authorities, paid for their members' funerals and provided aid to orphans, settled controversies among members, and inflicted fines and sometimes even expulsions. They offered the cities memorable feasts and commissioned works of art and devotion for the guild "schools". Teaching was carried out inside the community, in which apprentices learnt not only the skills necessary to undertake socially recognized activities but also the principles inspiring those activities, the goals and responsibilities they involved.

The model of a school as a community set of practices has been supplanted in modern Western societies by another model, that of an organization which is reduced simply to transmitting information. This new model has the advantage of ignoring the moral dimension of education, which is increasingly difficult to manage in a society in which diverse, conflicting cultures meet and confront each other. This convenient solution can count on two extraordinarily powerful allies. One is the first wave in cognitive psychology, from Herbert Simon to Allen Newell, which reduces human knowledge to simple information processing (for a different cognitive approach, see Mantovani, 1996a). The other ally is the "information society revolution" which developed in the 1980s with the advent of the personal computer. The two processes are so closely entwined that they cannot really be distinguished. They have in common the erroneous yet insidiously persuasive idea that information is knowledge.

This notion simplifies every educational task to an extraordinary degree. On 12 April 1999, my usual newspaper (*La Repubblica*) carried a multimedial software advert which ran something like this:

> Learn to write with a reader which repeats the words you key in on the computer! Construct your own personalized encyclopedia on CD-ROM, linking words, definitions and images! Get to know grammar with a video game, play dominoes with words, in an environment full of fascinating sounds and colours! These are not the impossible dreams of science fiction, but examples of what is happening in schools today, thanks to the meeting of education with new technologies. Over 3,500 schools are already on the Internet. By the year 2000, 15,000 more will have multimedial inputs!

This is not a dream, it's a nightmare: the idea that, right from the start, an imposing multimedial arsenal, not simple even for an adult to manage, is erected between a child and that same child's learning how to write. The fact that electronic systems tend to be "obscure" to their users – because they work in ways which are not intuitively transparent – does not generally facilitate sense-making in computerized environments (Weick, 1990). This is why we may expect that learning how to write by computer will pose peculiar problems, and we will have to study the advantages and disadvantages of the new learning environments. Instead of facing this sort of problem in a serene manner, the mass media prefer to say what informatics marketing wants people to think.

The nightmarish article continued with a blare of trumpets: "The multi-medial revolution is invading all school life! While old controversies on the backwardness of school curricula drag on, a myriad of new projects is coming into being! The most ambitious of these is Minister X's plan for telematics and CD-ROMs in every classroom, billions of lire will be invested!" The figure of the teacher, as opposed to that of the computer, has disappeared completely; the triumphal entry of the marvellous knowledge-machines into schools will solve education's problems once and for all. We do favour the new technologies – we have been studying them for years – but for this very reason we find the way the media presents them highly misleading. Superficiality is not useful when difficult tasks have to be faced. Many researches show that introducing computers into organizations tends to widen the gap between those who have and those who do not have means, competences and resources. For schools, this would be a real tragedy.

We are told in the above advert that controversies on obsolete school curricula are over. It is not clear whether this means that multimediality is an innovative curriculum in itself, as such replacing previous programs, or whether the controversies are no longer necessary because the software egg-heads have already made the right choices and so there is nothing left to discuss. The triumphal tone of the advert is characteristic of the peculiar rhetorical genre which Rob Kling (1994) calls "technological utopianism", which deeply affects the technological approach to education. Nicholas Negroponte, head of MIT's Media Lab, in his bestseller *Being Digital* (1995), writes:

> While the politicians struggle with the baggage of history, a new generation is emerging from the digital landscape free of many of the old prejudices. These kids are released from the limitations of geographic proximity as the sole basis of friendship, collaboration, play, and neighborhood. Digital technology can be a natural force drawing people into greater world harmony.
>
> (Negroponte, 1995: 230)

What Negroponte is saying is: provide information and you will have knowledge – knowledge free from the complications of history and the vileness of politics. Computers pretend to offer young people access to a world of peace and harmony; in fact they offer a world in which Aunt Itka's bandage is an insignificant detail of a forgotten past. Negroponte says that young people are free from memory, a useless burden which adults can be left to carry. The chasm between young people and adults, between the restraints of history and the freedom of "being digital", between the prejudices of the past and the exhilarating knowledge accessible via computer networks is the core of the technological approach to education.

THE CULTURAL MODEL

The cultural (as opposed to the informational) concept of education does not underrate the importance of the new technologies. It sees education as a process triggered off by cultural transmission, aiming at the construction of meanings (see Note 3). It is comforting to see how this perspective is gaining ground even among computer scientists (Clancey, 1994, 1997). The May 1997 issue of *Communications of the ACM*, organ of the Association for Computing Machinery, with 84,000 members worldwide, carried an article by Soloway and Wallace (1997), criticizing aspects of the current educational use of the World Wide Web which, at the end of 1996, had about 50 million pages and which is growing at a vertiginous pace every day. What a mine of information!

If information were knowledge, the Web would be Aladdin's cave for anyone who wanted to learn anything under the sun. But it is not. And why not? Because, answer Soloway and Wallace,

> while 'ask-the-expert' sites surely do have a place on the Web, they are in no way a panacea for learning. If we are going to prepare our children for the demands of the workplace and the demands of citizenry in a democratic, global community, then we must help them move beyond thinking that answers to questions can be simply found. Rather, answers need to be constructed and synthesized, from all manner of resources.
>
> (Soloway and Wallace, 1997: 16)

Knowledge is a personal enterprise, an exploration guided by maps which culture makes available to its members to orient them in their search. What a pity it would be if the opportunities offered by the new information technologies were wasted because of a base idea of learning encouraging young people to "find" ready-made answers to their questions in the Web!

The concept of education as a cultural process (Note 7) enhances history and memory, which Negroponte equates to the machinations of politicians. History is the heritage transmitted by adults and elders to the younger members of a community. It is within this framework that older people are important, as highlighted by Firth (1960), an American anthropologist who worked in Polynesia in the first half of the twentieth century. He reports some touching scenes of cultural transmission captured during his field work on the island of Tikopia:

> When a chief imparts his knowledge to his son while still young and vigorous he always leaves a few things unrevealed until the time comes when he can no longer walk about. Then he tells his son to come and he pillows his head under his father's arm. The chief covers them both with one blanket and tells him finally all the formulae of the *kava* and other sacred things.
>
> (Firth, 1960: 28)

The right person, the person whose duty it is, receives a legacy handed down to him by and from his remote ancestors. This teaching identifies the person, and his rank and tasks inside his social group. Strength, power and status are passed from the old man to his son, perfecting his identity as a man, a member of his group, and a leader. The old man has custody of the rituals, principles and values of the community. After having revealed his secrets to his son, the father asks him to repeat them: it would be terrible if they were transmitted in an inaccurate or distorted manner. "Then he [the old man] asks his son, 'Now you tell me that I may listen and see if it is complete'. The son repeats all he knows while the father corrects him and makes additions. When the chief is satisfied he says to his son, 'Now, all your things are complete'" (Firth, 1960: 28).

What is complete? Why does the old man now believe that he has fulfilled his task? Because only now does he know that he has transmitted what he himself received and what identifies him as a man: rules of living and the ideals of his community; the capacity to distinguish not only between right and wrong (which is already quite something), but also between what is beautiful and what is not, between enthusiasm and brutality, sincerity and crudity. The object of cultural transmission is not a set of commands or a code of conduct like that invoked by the Lexington spokeswoman, but a system of principles gracefully embodied in practices. Our culture tells us what to do, how and why: what marriage is, why and how to celebrate a wedding, and even how to prepare the wedding breakfast.

The more the son receives of the culture of his community, the more he will be able to use it as a personal intimate resource. Stanner (1960) describes the effects of initiation on Durmugam, a North Australian aborigine he met during his field work:

> Durmugam was initiated, as he says, 'in the bush', at a time when a relatively large number of aborigines could be assembled and the full panoply of ceremonial forms could be followed. He emerged a

blackfellow for life. He did not simply reach manhood; he was *given* it, was *made* a man by men who stood for and taught him to stand for a tradition in part only revealed. Later he learned the full tradition, not of his own, but of neighbourly tribes."

(Stanner, 1960: 95)

Durmugam received only partial initiation because there was no longer anyone who could transmit his people's traditions in an exhaustive fashion. There were too few old people, and those few could not complete his initiation. Yet he could not do without it, because:

The initiation teaches boys to be men; to know pain and to ignore it; to feel fear and master it; to want, but to bear the necessary costs; to grasp that outside society they are nothing – in the isolation of initiation they are called 'wild dogs' – and, inside it, masters; that through them The Dreaming is 'followed up'; that the tradition is 'The Road'.

(Stanner, 1960: 95)

The lack of appropriate cultural transmission does not produce independence and freedom, it produces frustration and rage. Twenty years after his first incomplete initiation, Durmugam lives in an environment devastated by utter and uncontrolled conflict:

No one dared to walk about alone. To do so invited speculation about evil motives, or risked the assassin's spear. An unescorted woman was usually raped. Men, even within eyeshot of their camps, carried a *womerah*; it suggested pacific intention but gave them a means of returning a spear. If they went any distance they carried a spear as well. The camps were fenced in with wire-netting or scraps of roof-iron. No one slept close enough to the fence to be within reach of a warlock's arm.

(Stanner, 1960: 83)

The hostility and paranoia pervading a community in such a state that it can no longer assign plausible meaning to events recalls the desolate outskirts of our mega-cities where ferocious gangs of youths have nothing better to do than plan mayhem. We see their violence on TV, so that the actions of a few criminals can invade the minds of the millions of people who watch "the box". Day after day, evening after evening, children witness on their TV screens infinite killings, rapes and acts of violence, and what do they dream of when they go to bed, what do they talk about the next morning? How can we remove the impression that Virgil's handcuffs are the response of a society which is so bewildered and frightened by the eradication of its cultural memories and by the lack of shared moral principles that it is only capable of punishing its victims?

Chapter 12

Crossing borders

BEING DIGITAL

During the 1968 student revolt in Paris, the originally attractive slogan "*L'imagination au pouvoir!*" ("Power to the imagination!") was immediately belied by barricades, cars in flames, and tear-gas: a scenario which smacked of *déjà vu* in a city like Paris where every stone recalls the bloody struggles to create modern France, from the Bastille to the Commune, and ancient battles, when the medieval city rose against feudal cavaliers and barred the streets with iron chains to prevent their passage. That is, there was not much imagination around. There were only tiny pieces of power: some of the young rebels later became officially respected *maitres à penser*, with their cosy little jobs in the sumptuous palaces of power.

The fiery propagandists of the new technologies also appeal to our imagination and thirst for novelty, assuring us that the Internet, interactive TV, multimediality and so on mark the beginning of an era of freedom, harmony and creativity for all. The "impact" of technology on society is the most frequently used metaphor, conjuring up visions of salvoes of prodigious missiles homing in on an inert, prostrate social body and galvanizing it into renewed life and vigour. This popular metaphor is in fact deeply misleading: society creates technologies, not vice versa.

Negroponte (1995) again assures us: "The harmonizing effect of being digital is already apparent as previously partitioned disciplines and enterprises find themselves collaborating, not competing. A previously missing common language emerges, allowing people to understand across boundaries. Kids at school today experience the opportunity to look at the same thing from many perspectives" (Negroponte, 1995: 230). It is not clear how electronics can stimulate the development of "many perspectives" in education, which are the result, surely, of the opposite, cultural, approach.

The biblical promise of a land flowing with milk and honey pales when compared with the scenario which Negroponte announces as imminent:

But more than anything, my optimism comes from the empowering nature of being digital. The access, the mobility, and the ability to effect change are what will make the future so different from the present. The information superhighway may be mostly hype today, but it is an understatement about tomorrow. It will exist beyond people's wildest predictions. As children appropriate a global information resource, and as they discover that only adults need learner's permits, we are bound to find new hope and dignity in places where very little existed before.

(Negroponte, 1995: 231)

A future incomparably brighter than the present grey dullness: young people who never need to ask anything, adults whose role is now simply to take a back seat and not to interfere. Dignity for all along information superhighways: brazen publicity at the service of aggressive marketing techniques. Is any of this true? Let's consider Negroponte's first statement, that electronic technologies will break down the barriers between different scientific disciplines. This would certainly be an important achievement since, as we have seen, scientific disciplines and new professions are increasingly becoming cultures in their own right; to reverse this trend would be a considerable exploit.

But this is not generally the case. Philip Agre, of the University of California, Los Angeles, one of the most original computer scientists of today, recalls his formative years as a young scientist at the MIT: "When I was a graduate student in Artificial Intelligence, the humanities were not held in high regard. They were vague and woolly, they employed impenetrable jargons, and they engaged in 'meta-level bickering that never decides anything'" (Agre, 1995: 1) Instead of opening up barriers between different disciplines, in the Artificial Intelligence laboratory attempts were purposely made to make those barriers more robust:

> Although my teachers and fellow students were almost unanimous in their contempt for the social sciences, several of them (not all, but many) were moved to apoplexy by philosophy. Periodically they would convene impromptu two-minute hate sessions to compare notes on the arrogance and futility of philosophy and its claims on the territory of AI research. 'They've had two thousand years and look what they've accomplished. Now it's our turn.' 'Anything that you can't explain in five minutes probably isn't worth knowing'.
>
> (Agre, 1995: 1)

Why so much hate? There was no fear of competition, philosophers did not threaten the development of Artificial Intelligence as an autonomous discipline. What was upsetting for Artificial Intelligence scientists was the different way of thinking which was present in other disciplines:

They distinguished between 'just talking' and 'doing', where 'doing' meant proving mathematical theorems and writing computer programs. A new graduate student in our laboratory, hearing of my interest in philosophy, once sat me down and asked in all seriousness, 'Is it true that you don't actually do anything, that you just say how things are?' It was not, in fact, true, but I felt with great force the threat of ostracism implicit in the notion that I was 'Not doing any real work'.

(Agre, 1995: 1)

Ancestors would have starved to death if they had had to depend for their nourishment on the Stanford scientists in Artificial Intelligence.

Agre describes the impermeable borders of his discipline: "Arguments and criticisms from outside the field can make no claim at all against it." The entire rising discipline of Artificial Intelligence seemed to him to round out for itself an isolated field of knowledge:

The substance of the field consists of the 'state of the art' and its history is a history of computer programs. The technical methods underlying these programs might have originated in other fields, but the real work consisted in formalizing, elaborating, implementing, and testing these ideas. Fields which do not engage in these painstaking activities, it is said, are sterile debating societies which do not possess the intellectual tools – most particularly mathematics – to do more than gesture in the general direction of an idea, as opposed to really working on it.

(Agre, 1995: 1)

This young community had aspects which, from some points of view, recall that difficulty in recognizing the existence of the other that we encountered in Columbus's ritual of "taking possession" of the New World.

SUBMERGED BY MESSAGES

Professions, especially the new ones which have to confront consolidated traditions, erect their own barriers against others and add them to the old ones founded on race, religion, caste and class. New prejudices overlap old ones: adults are portrayed as the ignorant savages of the new informatic world. Their knowledge and experience are worth nothing. Negroponte (1995) sneers at them: they need a learner's permit, he says, while the young are lucky; for them there is the thrill of breathtaking rides along electronic superhighways. Adulation of the young and denigration of adults are cardinal features of the new mystique which sets Internet against history, future against past, young against old, and, once again, launches the fascinating slogan *"L'imagination au pouvoir!"* But there can be no imagination without roots, only the aspirations of a petty power.

Informational technologies in themselves, in spite of specious publicity campaigns which would have us believe the contrary, are not the answer to social problems. In fact, they can *create* problems, because society is often not prepared to use them properly, that is as tools for recognizable and valuable social projects (Mantovani, 1994, 1995, 1996a; Mantovani and Riva, 1999). Technologists can make useful contributions if they understand the questions society poses, but only if they learn to collaborate with others and respect their competence. From this viewpoint, persisting prejudices against the social sciences are a severe cultural limitation for which the development of the new technologies is paying a very high price.

And what about the contribution of new technologies to freer, richer communications? The new environments do offer considerable opportunities, but they are not simple to introduce: communications are faster, but they submerge us. Since information is not in itself knowledge, but at best something we must work on to produce knowledge, the information overload hinders the development of high-level cognitive processes, which requires time and attention. Although expert users have often developed personal strategies to avoid being drowned under the rising tide of information overload, they too suffer from considerable tension.

Here is the text of the automatic answer message I received the other day from a colleague:

> Hi. I was at XY State University for a public lecture and discussion and diverse seminars w/faculty & students. I'll try to respond to your email by late next week. My various folders now have about 1470 messages to respond to your message will come into the inbox above position 263 (see inbox below). I received 143 email messages between Tues–Thurs. 40 messages came in between 3:40PM on Thurs & 8:30 on Friday. I will try to reply to yours promptly ... all things considered. And was drowned w/ more mail on Sat & Monday. ... There has been some email progress here ... two weeks ago, despite daily efforts to respond to incoming and other key email my daily average hovered around 1400. I pruned it down to 1370 before I left on this trip. I estimated it would be around 1470–1520 by Friday AM. It reached 1450 (after pruning a few) by Thursday 1:51PM. By Saturday I was down to 1425 messages but up to 1470 on Monday, despite answering many messages. I hope to get to yours soon.

The message continues with yet further details on the overwhelming flood of messages my friend has to absorb, with all the e-mail folders automatically updated by a special program. Used like this, e-mail can create some problems; all I needed was something like: "Hi, I'm well, I'll be in touch with you later", instead of this mass of numbers. But my friend has to give me all this information in order to justify his delay in responding, because e-mail etiquette requires him to answer immediately if not sooner, and the pressure to do so is considerable. I know perfectly well that preparing a response requires time, but this obvious consideration comes nowhere in a context obsessed with the myth of speed at all costs.

BEING CULTURAL

Along our way in this metaphor of a journey, of exploration of the real world, which has accompanied us from the beginning of this work and has grown with us step by step, we now come to a crossroads, or rather a T-junction. We can imagine the future either *à la* Negroponte or according to the view presented here. If we heed Aunt Itka's bandage with its patrimony of history, memory and reflection, we choose the cultural pathway; if we jettison the past in order to race free from the "baggage of history" along informational highways, we take the other. We have two different perspectives on understanding personal responsibility, methods of working, and ways of organizing time and commitments. Philip Agre has shown us that the contrast is not between technology and culture, but between different ways of seeing both. As a young scientist at MIT, Agre did really brilliant scientific work, but some members of his community thought he was more interested in theories than in writing computer programs. He risked ostracism, like Alvar Nuñez, and for the same reasons.

The difference between Philip Agre and his colleagues was not that he was a philosopher in disguise and they were true scientists. The difference lay in their ways of viewing science, technology and society (Agre, 1997). When technology does not forget Aunt Itka's bandage and similar insignificant details up to Colombus's "taking possession" of the New World and even further, then technology lies within society, it is a tool for enhancing memory and education. But when, in the name of technology, puerile utopias are arrayed before us – suggesting, for instance, that the problems of school and education can be resolved through access to the Internet and through intense use of multimedial tools – technology is degraded to the level of a money-making machine at the expense of the unwary.

At our crossroads, we can turn left. We can believe that the more information we can stash away the richer our future will be. We can float in an ocean of external stimuli. We can let ourselves be "consumed by the social connection", as Gergen (1991) writes in his book on *The Saturated Self*, in which he reports the nightmare of an ordinary working day:

> I had just returned from a two-day conference in Washington, which
> had brought together fifty scholars from around the country. An urgent

fax from Spain lay on the desk, asking about a paper I was months late in contributing to a conference in Barcelona. Before I could think about answering, the office hours I had postponed began. One of my favorite students arrived and began to quiz me about the ethnic biases in my course syllabus. My secretary came in holding a sheaf of telephone messages, and some accumulated mail, including an IRS notice of a tax audit and a cancellation notice from the telephone company. . . . By the morning's end I was drained. The hours had been wholly consumed by the process of relating – face to face, electronically, and by letter. The relations were scattered across Europe and America, and scattered points in my personal past. And so keen was the competition for 'relational time' that virtually none of the interchanges seemed effective in the ways I wished.

(Gergen, 1991: 1)

Nor do things improve after lunch: two hours of lessons, a visit from a Chicago colleague, a departmental meeting and more meetings with students close in upon Gergen before he finally goes home in the evening, only to find another load of mail there too, his family wanting to give and receive information, the telephone, the newspaper, the TV – and the lawn, which needs mowing. Gergen compares the stimuli he has received during an ordinary working day with those of his childhood, spent in a peaceful little town in North Carolina in the early 1950s. There there is no common measure. With respect to a past which is still quite recent, our present world is crammed full of information to be digested.

Gergen notes that there is so little time for interchange that "none of the interchanges seemed effective" in the ways he wished. Informational overload is accompanied by a sense of dissatisfaction at the low quality of those interchanges. If more information did in fact equal more knowledge, our society would be the wisest in human history and we would be the most sapient of beings. But we are confused, "saturated" in Gergen's words. We do not have enough time, either to digest information provided by the "outside" world or to generate knowledge stemming from "inside", surfacing in our memories thanks to silence and reflection.

So, when we reach our crossroads, let us turn right and avoid overtaxing our brains by loading them with unwanted information. Let us adjust our relationships with the environment so that they are controlled and purposeful. Let us refuse to rush at things, because we will inevitably end up doing them badly. If we treat situations in standardized ways, we lose sight of their uniqueness, that is, their cultural specificity. Culture, as we have seen, is the capacity to see boundaries and to have the courage to pass over them, like Alvar Nuñez. As we do too, every time we dare to take time off to reflect quietly and to use our imaginations to escape from boxed-in, stereotyped schemes. This requires time for pondering: Alvar

Nuñez could never have become a shaman after only a week's "full immersion".

The right-hand turn leads us to the "estranged man" (*l' homme dépaysé*), the expression that Tzetan Todorov (1996) uses to indicate a person who was born in one culture but who is also part of another. His own experience was that of a Bulgarian transplanted to Paris:

> I was an immigrant, a Bulgarian in France. I had to yield in the face of the evidence, I would never be a Frenchman like the others. Even the woman I had married on the eve of my departure for Bulgaria [it was Todorov's first journey home after eighteen years' absence] was, like me, a foreigner in France. My actual state does not correspond either to deculturation or to acculturation, but is something I could call transculturation, the acquisition of a new code without the loss of a previous one. I live in a peculiar space: I am a foreigner 'at home' (in Sofia) and at home 'abroad' (in Paris).
>
> (Todorov, 1996: 13)

EXPANDING OUR EXPERIENCE

Any person born in one society who enters into contact with another discovers, like Renato Rosaldo among the Ilingot headhunters, that his moral standards are not absolute. However, the bewilderment produced by taking the other seriously is repaid by a widening of the confines of our experience. Todorov gives us this idea of a man free of nostalgia for his native country: "Today the exile is the person who, modifying the original sense, best embodies the ideal formulated by Ugo de Saint Victor in the twelfth century: The man who finds his country sweet is only a babe-in-arms; he for whom every land is like his own is already full-grown; but the perfect man is he for whom the whole world is but a foreign country' " (Todorov, 1996: 13).

The image of the exile enhances our metaphor of the journey: each person is travelling towards an unknown horizon. Although in a certain sense the journey is embedded in its very beginning, in the maps provided before departure, in fact it leads the wanderer into unexplored territories. His eyes and mind, accustomed to received maps, find it difficult to register novelties. The map of the Pyrenees can be used to find one's way in the Alps, and it will be corrected as one stumbles along. We are constantly obliged to use the sense-making grid that our culture has given us, but at the same time we have to transcend it, re-interpret it, adapt it to surrounding reality.

The worst thing for tradition is to be preserved in a glass case, like a stuffed animal. In this sense Western culture too, apparently the winner on a world scale, is a net with holes in it. A net which, more than others, must continually expand to contain the new experiences which are caught in it. It cannot refuse to receive them, it would dry up and die. Roots reveal their power in the tree which towers above them; the strength of a culture manifests itself in its capacity to accept other worlds and to open its members' minds and wills to see differences and appreciate them, although at first this may seem disorienting.

The new frontier is not that of constructing increasingly powerful machinery and becoming used to swallowing down incredible doses of information, but that of learning how to set aside time for reflection. Many have given up this quest; they say things like: "I am no longer master of my time", "I am buried under loads of information", "I can't cope with it all". This is a sure sign of deep disorder: these people have lost control not only of their actions but also of their thoughts. If they haven't got time to think, what can they add to that frantic to-ing and fro-ing of information which takes up so much of that same time?

Dwelling on this new frontier will help us to avoid other Bosnias, Kosovos, other *Shoah* and other gulags. The past cannot be visited in a triumphalistic manner. The need to abandon an imperialistic vision of culture applies to history too, since history is the core of culture. Todorov (1996), referring to the Balkan wars which bloodied Europe and indeed the world for almost a century, writes:

> Collective memory in general prefers to conserve two types of past situations: those in which we were victorious heroes, and those in which we were innocent victims. Both may serve to substantiate our present claims. But those situations, which may really have existed, help to blind us to the present rather than open our eyes to it. The least glorious pages of our past would be the most instructive if we applied ourselves to reading them thoroughly. The past is fruitful not when it serves to nourish resentment but when its bitter taste drives us to transform ourselves.
> (Todorov, 1996: 49)

We need only look around to see that this task is still to be carried out.

A school which offered CD-ROMs in every classroom but which did not know how to arouse in its students an interest in history, a passion for reading, a love for art and nature would, at most, produce nothing but *idiots savants*, little smart-asses only capable of participating in TV quiz shows, clad in brand-new clothes with their hair slicked down, prompt with answers to questions like: "Which city is the Sistine Chapel in?". If even mature minds run the risk of burn-out due to informational overload, what will be the mental health of young minds to whom the mass media, slaves to informatics marketing, explain incessantly that you can find everything and more besides on the Internet? Who will explain to them that "interacting" is not enough, that you must use your brain as well?

True journeys require imagination, courage and attention. Here is Robert

Byron's description of his journey in Oxiana – a region stretched over the borders between Iran and Afghanistan – in the thirties:

> Small clouds are shining in the blue. We rise by gentle slopes to a panorama of dun rolling country, chequered with red and black plough, and sheltering grey, turreted villages in its folds; breaking against the far mountains into hills streaked with pink and lemon; bounded at last by range upon range of jagged lilac. The twin peaks above Tabriz go with us. So do a flight of yellow butterflies. Far below a horseman approaches. 'Peace to you.' 'Peace to you.' Clip, clop, clip, clop, clip, clop . . . We are alone again.
>
> (Byron, 1937 [1992]: 79)

The suspended, enchanted atmosphere of this scene should not deceive us. The journey is not always so easy. The flocks of yellow butterflies and the small clouds in the sky are the exception, not the rule. The rule is the hardness of the path and the determination to continue:

> Then on, against the wind and wet, over the grey hummocky wastes. The grey zeppelin clouds drive low and fast. The grey infrequent villages are desolate of people. Clustering round their ruined citadels, those ancient shapes, the bee-hive dome and ziggurat, are melting in the rain. They have melted thus since the dawn of history; and when summer comes, they will rise again out of new mud bricks till history closes. Streams in purple spate swirl through the walled lanes into the fields, and out into the desert. The track itself becomes a watercourse. In a night, the poplars have lost their leaves, though the planes hold theirs for a day more. Strings of camels sway alongside us – boom goes the bull-camel's bell – boom, and it is gone. Shepherds in white tabards tack through the gale after pebble-grazing flocks.
>
> (Byron, 1937 [1992]: 79)

This image of the journey far from home is only apparently the opposite of domestic cultural transmission; in reality, it is its other face. The maps of our tradition were given to us to explore reality and the fruits of our explorations are the tales of new things we have seen thanks to those maps and, in some cases, in spite of them. At the end of our journey, we will not find ourselves so far from our starting point as we had supposed, but we will have had the opportunity to develop greater understanding of the advantages and limitations of the maps which guided us. And we will be able to hand them down, revised and updated, to those about to begin their journeys, if they wish.

Conclusions

In this book, we have gradually, step by step, focused our eyes on parts of the invisible elephant of the Introduction. At every stage, our view of culture has been enriched with some element: starting from culture as a framework organizing individual experience, we measured the extent of the differences which separate cultures, and examined the three functions which culture fulfils in human societies. At the end we spoke about education. Post-modern societies – deeply disoriented by the strain of globalization processes and the flood of information they receive without being given time and tools to assimilate it – need space for memory, in order to reflect on their own history and on their encounters with others. Each community exploits its own history in order to reconstruct its identity and recognize the reasons of others.

We can now perceive the silhouette of the previously invisible elephant, although it is still a little hazy. We still cannot distinguish the dragon-fly which accompanies it, the variations arising in the framework of traditional order, like the pale pink chador of a girl in Iran, like an engineering professor reading a book on cultural psychology like this, or a sixteenth-century *conquistador* becoming a shaman like Alvar Nuñez. These things are improbable but not impossible: on the contrary, they are events which occur and, when they do, they make us appreciate the unexpected mingling of tradition and novelty. True, in Iran once various colours of chador could be worn, and they were often pale pink and not black – the innovation we imagined above as something strange and unexpected is something that really happened in the past. Sometimes imagination re-invents tradition and often tradition encourages imagination.

And yet culture remains, for most of us, a huge elephant, the imposing collective patrimony of tradition, as opposed to the flexible creativity of the individual. It is difficult to see how traditional principles and individual variations, social rules and personal improvisation, can mingle. And yet we cannot innovate unless we start from a pre-existing repertory. Culture is not outside, around or above people, but within them, the core of their personal identity. Attitudes, judgements and prejudices sink their roots in the history of a society which its members constantly reprocess, giving it new forms.

One image quoted above clearly sums up the nature, at the same moment public and private, of culture: the conversation which began before we arrived and which continues after we leave. In it, sense-making is based on stories heard and told, stories which tell us not only what happened but also what should have happened: interesting stories have important moral aspects. Conversation is not simply an interpersonal exchange regulated by mechanisms defining whose turn it is to speak, how messages can be acknowledged, and so on; it is a form of social construction of reality. It is not language in its abstract sense but situated discourse which is the privileged tool of cultural mediation; cultural practices and beliefs are produced and transmitted in the context of a speaking community (Duranti, 1997).

I have given a narrative tone to my discourse to involve readers in sense-making, in moral interrogation, in curiosity about exemplar stories, like that of Alvar Nuñez wandering naked and lost among the swamps and shores of Florida or that of Renato Rosaldo discussing the Vietnam war and head-hunting with his Ilingot friends. Narration is an educational tool – education being understood as a process of cultural transmission, not just the transfer of information from an expert who delivers a carbon copy of what they already know to an ignorant novice.

The travel metaphor – adventures, maps and frontiers – used here has the disadvantage of suggesting that "new" is faraway, that "the other" lives somewhere else. We have spoken of the need to accept "others" and their cultural identity, but we have not said that "others" are often no longer such because, before us, they have travelled along a lengthy stretch of road to reach us. They have become "us" to the point of incorporating important parts of our culture, as Alvar Nuñez did when he became one of "them", the Indios, for seven years.

An example: in Italy, while some leaders of the 1968 student revolt were demanding that Dante's works should be expunged from high-school programmes and, if possible, even from university curricula as relics of the Medieval past, in Japan a man was reading *The Divine Comedy* and feeling that this reading was important in his formation. A sophisticated whim, like buying a Gucci handbag or an Armani suit? No, simply an effect of cultural transmission: when that man was a child, his grandfather used to recite to him Dante's *Comedy* and others of his works.

The child was called Kenzaburo Oe, and he lived his early childhood among the horrors of war and the shock of occupation. He then began to write in a way which was new for his countrymen, without hiding his alcoholism, sexual disorders, and his rejection of his handicapped son Hikari, whom he later tenderly loved. Oe received the Nobel Prize for literature in 1994. He concludes his autobiographical novel *The Years of Nostalgia* (1987) quoting the five triplets of *The Divine Comedy* which describe the meeting between Dante and Casella, his musician friend, on the beach of the mountain of Purgatory. Casella sings for Dante "*Amor che ne la mente mi ragiona*" ("Love converses in my mind"), Dante's song from "*Il Canzoniere*" dear to them both, before leaving his friend and beginning his climb up the mountain of Purgatory.

Kei, the hero of the novel who takes the part of Oe, sets on these verses his memory of his dear friend Gii:

> Gii, I always think of this scene together with that of the island of the Majestic Hinoki. You are lying on the grass. A short distance away, Setsu and Asa are gathering grass. Then I notice that I too am lying on the ground beside you. Hikari and Yu have also come to cut grass. It is a radiantly beautiful day. The apple green of the willow buds and the intense green of the Majestic Hinoki glisten from the night's rain and set off the shimmering white masses of cherry blossom. Time passes slowly. A dignified old man appears, and scolds us: '*What is this, ye laggard spirits? What negligence, what stay is this? Run to the mountain to strip off the slough which lets not God be manifest to you.*' So, in all haste, we immediately began to run towards the foot of the Majestic Hinoki.
>
> (Oe, 1987: 211)

The old man who disturbs Oe's dream, interrupting his moment of happiness, is Cato, a Roman philosopher of the first century AD, who urges Dante and Casella to begin their purification immediately. Kenzaburo's grandfather recounted to his little grandchild, sitting entranced at his feet, the visions of a man who had lived centuries before on the other side of the world, and thus Dante, Casella and Cato entered Kenzaburo's mind, took their place in his memory, and populated his imagination. This reminds us of the Polynesian chief who transmits the secrets of his people to his son. Here, the grandfather tells his grandchild stories from the other side of the world. Who can speak of "us" and "them" in such a situation? We can only compliment ourselves on an encounter in which the "other" was no longer such. Oe goes on:

> But time passes in a circular way. And again you and I are lying on the grass of the meadow, Setsu and Asa are gathering grass, and Yu, like a little girl, and small, immaculate Hikari, whose handicap only enhances his innocent beauty, help them. The bright green of the Majestic Hinoki becomes even brighter, and the cascades of cherry blossom continue to float in the air. Until the old man returns, we will remain here on the fresh young meadow, in the balmy air of the island of the Majestic Hinoki.
>
> (Oe, 1987: 211)

The vision – that we received from Bakhtin – of culture as a kingdom all made of boundaries suggests to us that we can find ourselves only in our encounters with "others". Our home, our culture, dwells on boundaries. It is a place of meeting, of exchange, and of confrontation. Cultural identity is not a treasure to be jealously defended but an asset to be exchanged openhandedly.

Notes

1. Categorization and culture

Categorization is important for its central role both in cognition and in social life: through it, we classify every sort of object, other people and even ourselves. George Lakoff (1987) rejects the classical theories on the formation of categories using two arguments. The first comes from the work of Eleanor Rosch (1978) who studied the formation of "natural" categories, i.e., those referring to everyday objects and expressed in natural language. By doing this, Rosch gave a new turn to research on categorization, which had until then only dealt with artificial ultrasimplified objects such as large red triangles or small blue circles. She showed that assigning an object to a certain category depends on its distance from a central semantic core defined in terms of "prototype" rather than of common attributes: for example, a cow is a more "prototypical" member of the category "mammals" than a dolphin. Lakoff's second argument is that "basic level categories depend not on objects themselves, independent of people, but on the way people interact with objects: the way they perceive them, imagine them, organize information about them, and behave toward them with their bodies" (Lakoff, 1987: 51). Lakoff's concept of categories supports our cultural perspective. In Chapter 1, we see that, according to the Dyirbal categorization, birds are the spirits of dead women: experience and tradition mingle without leaving any residue, so that birds are perceived by the Dyirbal as spirits. In this text we will meet other similar cases of apparently strange categorizations, like the Christian leopard of the Dorze mentioned in Chapter 8, *Pride and dignity*. These cases show that we do not have two independent sources of knowledge, cultural tradition and "direct" experience, but a single experience which is culturally mediated by artifacts such as physical tools, pre-existing cultural beliefs, social norms, and so on.

Lakoff is aware of the key role of cultural dimension.

> What we call 'direct physical experience' is never merely a matter of having a body of a certain sort; rather, every experience takes place

within a vast background of cultural presuppositions. It can be misleading, therefore, to speak of direct physical experience as though there
were some core of immediate experience which we then 'interpret' in
terms of our conceptual system. Cultural assumptions, values, and attitudes are not a conceptual overlay which we may or may not place upon
experience as we choose. It would be more correct to say that all experience is cultural through and through, that we experience our 'world' in
such a way that our culture is already present in the very experience
itself.

(Lakoff and Johnson, 1980: 21)

This excerpt appears to accept the cultural dimension, but in the following lines a restriction is made on the ubiquity of cultural mediation:

However, even if we grant that every experience involves cultural presuppositions, we can still make the important distinction between
experiences that are 'more' physical, such as standing up, and those that
are 'more' cultural, such as participating in a wedding ceremony. When
we speak of 'physical' versus 'cultural' experience in what follows, it is
in this sense that we use the terms.

(Lakoff and Johnson, 1980: 21)

I am not totally in agreement with what is said in the second excerpt,
which presumes that some experiences are more cultural while others are
more physical. This line of separation seems to me difficult to draw: does it
make sense to consider standing up outside a precise cultural context, which
qualifies it and embodies a description of the correct way in which the act
itself should be carried out? Clearly, standing at a bus-stop or standing
during a military parade are culturally and physically very different. The
"physical" aspect of the experience is always embodied within its social,
cultural framework.

2. Categories in discourse

At one point in his book, George Lakoff (1987) complains that the most
boring aspect of teaching for a linguistics professor is being inveigled by
students into endless discussions on the 22 words (or more) which Eskimos
use to describe snow (this seems a problematic example). These 22 two
words, says Lakoff, tell us very little about the Eskimos' categorization system: "When an entire culture is expert in a domain they have a suitably large
vocabulary. It's no surprise, and it's no big deal. It is no more surprising than
that Americans have lots of names for cars" (Lakoff, 1987: 51) Derek
Edwards (1991), following the perspective of Discourse Analysis, criticizes
Lakoff's position by stating that categories are not descriptions of states of

things but essentially forms of discourse. "Categories are for talking", he says, they are created and used inside specific social contexts by people aiming at specific goals and at persuading themselves and others. Even if there were no important perceptual differences between the 22 types of Eskimo snow and the infinite number of types of cars which travel the length and breadth of the United States, the fact that different words are used cannot be ignored from the discursive and social points of view, because people use words precisely to segment and order reality and to mark membership of or exclusion from groups, as Sacks (1992) showed in his analysis of how Californian teenagers taking part in group therapy used the opposition between the illegally fast "hotrodder" and the placid "Pontiac station wagon" to define people inside or outside the group ("Pontiac station wagon", mom's car, was obviously a burning insult).

What might seem irrelevant from an abstract cognitive viewpoint may be important in the socially situated discourse and in the society which produces it.

> The various makes and marques of motor cars carry powerful semiotic significances, over and above perceptual distinctiveness and bodily use, and it is no great insight to suggest that it is precisely for such significances, for what it means to own and drive a Porsche, a safety-conscious Volvo or the top-of-the-range model within a fleet of company cars, that the different models are produced, badged and marketed. For motor cars, the categories may well exist, in just the way they exist, and are named, so that they can be socially deployed, such that it is only the fact of their perceptual distinctiveness which is trivial.
>
> (Edwards, 1991: 526)

Commenting on Borges' Chinese catalogue presented in Chapter 1, *Birds and spirits*, we noted that different categorizations of a given set of objects or events are possible according to the interests of the actors and the characteristics of the situations in question. Edwards too emphasizes the situated character of categories:

> The idea that semantic categories have fuzzy membership boundaries, inequities of membership and permit multiple and even contrasting possibilities for description suggests that language's category system functions not simply for organizing our understanding of the world but for talking about it in ways that are adaptable to the situated requirements of description, and to differences of perspective, and to the need to put words to work in the pragmatics of social interaction.
>
> (Edwards, 1991: 526)

Discourse Analysis, a new line of research on communication processes, stresses the fact that discourse is a social practice which is morally non-neutral: "Because categorical descriptions involve choice, and are rhetoric-ally consequential, they also potentially display the speaker as positioned, interested and accountable in a loosely moral sense for how things are described, and for the interactional consequences of descriptions" (Edwards, 1991: 526). Discourse analysis contests the view of knowledge adopted by the early cognitivists: there are no "objective" data which are not constructed by means of social exchange (Edwards, 1997; Edwards and Potter, 1992; Potter, 1996; van Dijk, 1997). Like Discourse Analysis, Con-versation Analysis also roots conversation in social negotiation, in those intergroup relations which Tajfel (1981) studied and in the contexts which conversation contributes to structure (Drew and Heritage, 1992; Sacks, 1992; Schlegoff, 1993). Discourse is persuasive, situated, interested (Antaki, 1994). Billig places peculiar emphasis on its dialectic character, on the fact that the core of discourse is discussion with others and with oneself. He discards the idea that categorization may simplify cognitive activity: "Cate-gorization does not provide the basis of thinking in a simple sense. The automatic application of categories is the negation of thinking, in that it is essentially a thoughtless process" (Billig, 1987: 140). Billig's position on categories approaches the extreme: in his view, thinking means taking details seriously, avoiding empty generalizations, perceiving the ideological dilemmas which crowd everyday life but are usually ignored by social psychology, intent on hunting down its decontextualized ghosts.

Discourse Analysis rejects the "mentalist social cognition" – the indi-vidualistic vision of most of social psychology (Condor and Antaki, 1997) – and questions its basic tenets, from Attribution Theory (Edwards and Potter, 1993) to the classic concept of attitudes as stable and consistent individual characteristics (Potter and Wetherell, 1987). Although Discourse Analysis and cultural psychology stem from different roots, they do seem to march in the same direction. Discourse Analysis no longer shrouds itself in pure lin-guistic analysis, and cultural studies looks towards discourse as a special mediational tool.

3. Prejudice in discourse

The cultural approach to prejudice is neglected by current social psychology, due to its individualistic orientation. In Allport's classic definition of preju-dice as "an avertive or hostile attitude toward a person who belongs to a group, simply because he belongs to that group" (1954), prejudice is con-sidered as a particular case of attitude, the case in which the member of a dominant group manifests a negative attitude towards members of groups considered to be inferior. The roots of racism in the poisoned legacy of slavery in the United States, the crimes committed by the Nazi and Fascist regimes towards the Jews, the horrible Soviet machine which chewed up innocent people by the million for entire decades under Big Brother's wise guidance, all the collective atrocities we learn about every evening on our TV screens are beyond the scope of current social psychological research, which is involved only in individual affairs. In our text prejudice is first and foremost a social construction based on local culture and expressed through discursive practices (Potter and Wetherell, 1987). Wetherell and Potter (1988, 1992), studying the discourses of New Zealanders confronted with the claims of the Maori, the natives who were so long deprived of their rights in their own land by European colonists, show how prejudice can be recognized through analysis of the internal organization of discourse and of the ways in which the local social context enters discourse. Potter and Wetherell (1987) reject the traditional tenet in social psychology which considers attitudes as consistent and relatively stable individual dispositions ready to be translated into actions towards peculiar "objects of attitude". They criticize

> the customary view that attitudes are about distinct entities. Attitudes to immigrants, for instance, should concern an existing out-there-in-the-world group of people. Yet when we examined actual discourse, this simple 'word and object' view of attitudes became unworkable. It is clear that the attitudinal object can be constituted in alternative ways, and the person's evaluation is directed at these specific formulations rather than some abstract and idealized object.
>
> (Potter and Wetherell, 1987: 54)

In everyday life, they say, we do not find attitudes like "general afunctional decontextual principles" growing and thriving in the privacy of individual minds. Everyday situations are always special and people explore their "specialness" in discourse. Attitude in discourse is situated, sometimes even incoherent if the situation requires it. For the last fifteen years, Teun van Dijk, professor of Discourse Studies at the University of Amsterdam, has been studying the forms used to build ethnic prejudice in everyday life by analysing jokes and stories, news items, parliamentary debates, school textbooks and newspaper advertisements (1984, 1987, 1991, 1993a, 1993b). He stresses the fact that stories do not only reflect people's personal experiences but develop types of discourse fixed by social and cultural norms, genres which embody values and ideologies stemming from the heritage of a community.

4. Cultural psychology

Cultural psychology – A once and future discipline, is the title of Mike Cole's (1996) book dedicated to clarifying the theoretical roots of this old and fresh line of research. The history of cultural psychology (Jahoda, 1992, 1995) tells us that, at the dawn of modern scientific psychology, Wilhelm

Wundt devoted to it the last thirty years of his life, from 1890 to 1920, during which he wrote the ten volumes of his *Volkerpsychologie*. Wundt believed that study of "high-level" mental processes, i.e., those involving historical and social dimensions, should be the competence not of experimental psychology, which he considered only applicable to the most elementary psychic processes, but of another type of psychology. A second milestone in the history of cultural studies was the expedition promoted by the University of Cambridge in 1895 to the Torres Straits, which separate Australia from New Guinea. William Rivers presented the results of his studies on the natives' eyesight in the scientific report of the expedition, edited by its chief, Alfred Haddon (1901). Both methodological and theoretical aspects of the research were subjected to harsh criticism. Instead of quietening over the years, it has accompanied cross-cultural research until the present day. Mike Cole, who started his scientific career in the 1960s by taking part in a cross-cultural study on the development of memory in the children of the Kpelle rice-growers of central Liberia, later reached the conclusion that cross-cultural research was intrinsically flawed (Cole et al., 1971). In Cole's view (1990, 1996, 1999), culture cannot be considered as an independent variable, as in cross-cultural research, because there are no high-level processes which are immune from cultural influences. To search in different cultures for mechanisms which are supposed to be quantitatively differentiated but qualitatively identical – and which for this very reason can be studied by standard methods – presumes that psychic functions develop more or less in the same way across various cultures, so that comparisons are possible. Cross-cultural research starts from the hypothesis that, in the case in question, the Kpelle children classify, remember and organize their everyday experiences exactly as children in New England do, with quantitative but not qualitative differences. This is clearly not the case: what we consider normal for a child in American society incorporates the assumptions, for example, that that child goes to school at the age of six, that the school is of a certain type, etc. The influence of schooling cannot be ignored; culture is not, states Cole, an independent variable which we can manipulate. If the child goes to a certain type of school, has a certain type of family, living environment, and so on, that child will develop a certain way of classifying, remembering and reasoning. There is no cultural no man's land, there are no high-level processes which are free from cultural influences. Other cultural psychologists (del Rio and Alvarez, 1995; Holland et al., 1998; Shore, 1996; Valsiner, 1987, 1994, 1998; Wertsch, 1985, 1991, 1995) basically share Cole's criticism towards current cross-cultural research, although they do not express it too sharply. The pathway of cross-cultural research is at present quite different from that of cultural psychology (Malt, 1995; Bond and Smith, 1996). One of the most significant contributions in this area comes from Harry Triandis (1990), who has worked at length on the differences between individualistic and collectivistic cultures. He is aware of the intrinsic limitations of cross-cultural research and recognizes that the meaning of variables in field studies may sometimes not correspond to the meaning attributed to the measures by researchers but he believes that these shortcomings of cross-cultural research can be cured through suitable methodological procedures. Richard Shweder (1991, 1995; Shweder and Sullivan, 1990, 1993) emphasizes the depth of cultural differences: by reminding us that *suttee* is a heroic act in the Hindu world but a barely acceptable form of suicide in ours, he shows that cultures may sometimes be so far morally removed from each other that they are scarcely comprehensible. The image of culture which we have inherited from Bakhtin, that of a kingdom composed only of frontiers, with no territory inside them, conveys the general perspective of this volume, which plays on the double register of the ubiquity of cultural mediation (according to Cole) and of the radicality of differences (according to Shweder). Mike Cole teaches at the University of California, San Diego, where he founded and directs the Laboratory for Comparative Human Cognition which produces advanced educational tools like Fifth Dimension (Cole, 1996) and publishes an innovative journal, *Mind, Culture and Activity*. Vygotsky and the other "stars" of Soviet psychology, Luria (1979) and Leontiev (1978), played important roles in Cole's scientific formation, and he willingly admits his debt to them (Cole, 1990, 1995a, 1995b). From Mike Cole's work flows to us the vision of culture as a powerful mediation system: our relationship with the environment is mediated by artifacts which are always both material and conceptual.

5. Social constructionism

Discursive construction of reality, narrative construction of the self, social constructionism: Kenneth Gergen is a necessary point of reference for those who are interested in these topics. Gergen's criticism of the objectivistic tenets which control most of contemporary social psychology is refreshing: the social dimension of reality, he says, cannot be captured through a small number of over-simplified constructs (Gergen, 1989). In *Realities and Relationships – Soundings in Social Construction* (1994), Gergen presents the theoretical and historical bases of his approach to social psychology. The starting point is: "All that is meaningful grows from relationships". Mention of relationships does not have the limited sense of acknowledging that people often interact in everyday situations, but is intended to emphasize the fact that human experience is essentially constructed through relationships between people and their social and physical environments (this is also the view of Richard Lazarus (1991), another master of contemporary psychology). Meaning is not the product of isolated individuals. On the contrary, it originates inside a community whose members are able to negotiate it by referring to at least partially shared common ground:

> Discourse is not the possession of a single individual. Meaningful language is the product of social interdependence. It requires the coordinated actions of at least two persons, and until there is mutual agreement on the meaningful character of words, they fail to constitute language. If we follow this line of argument to its ineluctable conclusion, we find that it is not the mind of the single individual that provides whatever certitude we possess, but relationships of interdependency.
>
> (Gergen, 1994: viii)

In 1973, in his famous paper on '*Psychology as history*', Gergen boldly challenged the model of social psychology prevailing at that time. In 1972, an equally famous paper by Tajfel criticized the excessive individualism of current research in social psychology. In 1974, Harré questioned the usual setting of laboratory experiments: "Why not ask them?" – he queried – "Why not ask subjects (or better "participants" in social psychology experiments) what meaning they attribute to their acts?" Each of the three above mentioned papers sowed a seed which was to yield abundant fruit: Gergen's social constructionism, Tajfel's social identity theory, and Harré's ethogenic approach. Current critical social psychology sees in these papers of the early 1970s the starting point of the long pathway leading to its present state (Lubek, 1997; Spears, 1997). Gergen proposed history as a model for social sciences, considering it more suitable for understanding socio-historical processes than methods mimicking natural sciences in their effort to explain universal phenomena. Universality versus diversity: we find here the same contrast we saw in the preceding note, when we compared cross-cultural research and cultural psychology. Supporters of diversity conceive every situation as unique, produced by an unrepeatable series of events and encounters. In his works – from 'Narratives of the self', written with Mary Gergen in 1983, to 'If persons are texts' (1988), from the brilliantly innovative 'The saturated self' (1991) to the recent 'Technology and the self' (1996) – Kenneth Gergen highlights the erosion undergone by the stable identifiable self in advanced societies, a self which was previously the king-pin of psychological disciplines: "Under postmodern conditions, persons exist in a state of continuous construction and reconstruction; it is a world where anything goes that can be negotiated. Each reality of self gives way to reflexive questioning, irony, and ultimately the playful probing of yet another reality. The center fails to hold" (Gergen, 1994: 209). In this fluid situation, the narratives which construct the self become more and more precarious. When one of the participants in a relationship changes their narrative, by the same act the narratives of others are jeopardized – like a child who tells a mother: "You are not a good mum". "Identities, in this sense, are never individual; each is suspended in an array of precariously situated relationships" (Gergen, 1994: 209). We see identity as something that is constructed moment by moment in discourse, just like reality.

What does this term, "construction", mean? Paul Slovic (1995), a researcher on decision-making in uncertainty conditions, can help us by telling us this little story, which he found in Tversky and Thaler (1990), two other eminent cognitive psychologists (this string of quotations is in itself an interesting process of cultural transmission: it shows us that social constructionism has passed the frontiers of social psychology and now belongs to general psychologists too). Here is the story. Three baseball umpires are discussing fouls. The first says: "I call them as I see them". The second says: "I call them as they are". But the third says: "They ain't nothing till I call them". The first umpire thinks that calling a foul means perceiving and reporting it as correctly as possible ("I note that a foul has occurred within the limits of my visual field"). The second thinks that calling a foul is the result of objective mental processes ("I see a foul simply because a foul has been committed"). The third umpire, probably unwittingly, is a constructivist. He thinks that assessments are constructed in the process by means of which those same assessments are elicited. He might say: "The foul exists when I say it does, because I'm the umpire here and I have instruments allowing me to make it exist as a social fact; I may of course be wrong, but a foul is a foul only when I call it". We see that being a constructionist does not mean being a relativist – an accusation wrongly levied at Gergen – but being aware of the fact that we structure reality by means of our cultural grids. It means recognizing the ambiguity of everyday situations and the role played by artifacts in giving shape to our everyday experiences. Gergen's writings are constructionistic in the sense that: "They call attention to the multiplicity of ways in which 'the world' is, and can be, constructed" (Gergen, 1994: 82). This is not relativism, but awareness of the role of mediation in cognitive and social proceses; in this sense social constructionism can support our understanding of cultural mediation (Gergen et al., 1996)

6. Understanding mediation

Culture does not simply take on the task of supplying its members with physical and ideal artifacts allowing them to interact with their environment; it shapes the social and physical environment through its artifacts. In the constructivist view, the environment is not independent of its relationship with social actors: the foul exists the moment the umpire blows his whistle. Even "natural" environments reveal themselves, if we observe them closely enough, as cultural products. The panorama of the Dolomites in front of me is crammed with artifacts – from my window I can see many artificial objects such as cars, tractors, church belltowers, and so on. But the scene of the Dolomites is mediated in a deeper and more pervasive sense – it is the product of artifacts which are not tangible like tractors and belltowers, but whose effects are even more palpable: centuries-old documents are responsible for the lines which the boundaries of the fields and the edges of the forest follow; both ancient habits and modern rules establish when, how and how often one is allowed to go mushrooming or shooting in the woods; roe-deer and chamois skip up and down the steep slopes thanks to regional laws instituting and protecting parks. Above all, culture lies in the eye of the beholder, in my eye as I observe the roe-deer and chamois, the woods and the fields. It is both before my pupils, glasses and binoculars, as I follow the capering chamois or the grazing roe-deer, and (even more) behind my pupils, in the system of interests, values and expectations which direct my gaze. Until the spread of the Romantic movement, in Europe snow-covered peaks and wild mountains aroused no attention, excitement or feelings of delight, but were seen as desolate and hostile places, and woods were at most only good for huntsmen or recluses. When the way of viewing nature changed, the foreign travellers who ventured into the Alpine valleys filled their diaries with sublime inspirations aroused by the majestic summits of Mont Blanc and the Matterhorn (adding to their notes some mention of their disgust at the ways of the uncouth native population). Whether we like it or not, our sensibility and love for mountains and wilderness begins with Rousseau and continues with Messner. How can I distinguish what is "natural" from what is "cultural" in the landscape before my eyes? All human experience is culturally mediated and socially constructed; this situation is usually clarified through the "triangle of mediation" (Fig. 1).

The "triangle of mediation" implies that the relationship between subject and object, between mind and environment, is mediated by cultural artifacts, which are both physical and conceptual. This means that all human experience flows through mediation (Fig. 2)

There is in fact no chamois I can perceive "immediately": the very name I use to designate this shy and powerful beast is supplied by the cultural process, categorization, discussed in Chapter 1, *Birds and spirits*. The effect of this move is the disappearance of the "natural" object. There is no "natural" object as opposed to the mediated ones (Fig. 3); objects are just defined by the artifacts, physical and conceptual, which are used.

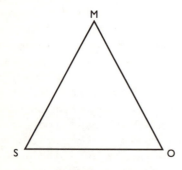

Figure 1   The basic triangle of mediation, in which subject (S) and object (O) are linked through a medium (M).

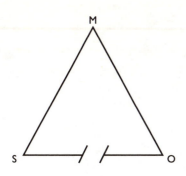

Figure 2 All experience is culturally mediated (M): the subject (S) has no direct access to the object (O).

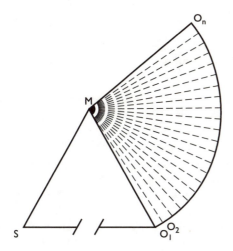

Figure 3 Mediation instruments define a range of possible objects ($O_1, O_2, \ldots O_n$).

Physical and social reality may well pre-exist the cultural filters through which I experience it, but my experience cannot avoid passing through those filters. The mountain peak now called "Croda Rossa" certainly existed long before my culture and my language came into being, but my experience of its beauty is only what my culture allows me. I do not have before my eyes a "natural" object, but a range of experiences mediated by physical (bin-oculars, photographs, mountain boots, climbers' ropes) and ideal tools (memories of the First World War, songs, tales told by the mountain guides, the modern feeling for nature) which I use in various ways compatible with the demands of my culture. A second effect of the change suggested in Figure 4 is that the subject, deprived of its anchor to a "natural" object, is also absorbed in the mediation process (Fig. 4).

As the object is experienced only in mediated form, the subject too is

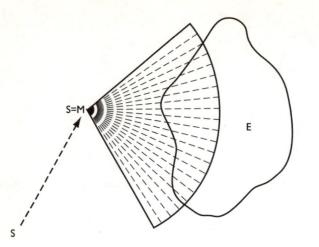

Figure 4 Subject (S) is not separate from the instruments of mediation (M), through which he/she constructs his/her environment and him/herself.

mediated by the narrative processes which construct and continuously reconstruct him/her (Gergen, 1994; Ochs 1997; Ochs and Capp, 1996). After the disappearance of subject and object as "natural" entities supposedly pre-existing mediation, of the original triangle only mediation remains. We could now speak no longer of "subject" and "object" but rather of social "actors" and of their "environments" (Fig. 5).

Figure 5 illustrates the passage from a dualistic unidirectional concept of the subject–object relationship (phase 1) to a still dualistic but bidirectional one (phase 2), up to the conception, proposed here, of relationship as a reciprocal construction (phase 3). The connection between this concept and recent developments in cognitive science (Situated Action Theory) is discussed in Mantovani (1996a). I merely state here that my perspective exploits as a precious resource the otherwise intractable intrinsic ambiguity of everyday situations that the studies of everyday cognition are now beginning to appreciate (Fig. 6).

Figure 6 shows how the actor–environment relationship is born in the encounter between the actor's interests (which are changeable and multiple, not necessarily coherent nor ordered on a stable scale of priorities) and the equally changeable and multiple affordances offered by the environment. This is a reciprocal construction, since the affordances present and at the same time latent in the environment are identified by the corresponding interests in the actor – interests which in turn are made salient and gain priority over other actors' interests due to the effect of the presence in the situation of the affordances appealing to them. The roots of the ambiguities of everyday situations lie in this extremely mobile co-construction which

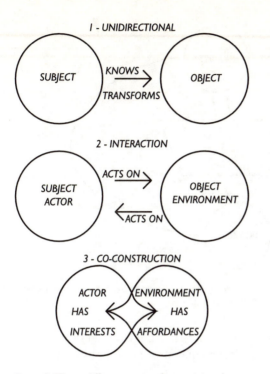

Figure 5 Three different ways of conceiving the actor–environment relationship.

Figure 6 The origin of the ambiguity of everyday situations in the actor–environment relationship (respectively A and E) and in the unpredictable meeting (*) between interests in A and affordances in E.

takes place between actors and their environments: situations may be interpreted in many ways according to the circumstances and the goals of the various actors involved (Fig. 7).

Figure 7 conveys the general sense of our discourse, which is that of showing how artifacts and principles intertwine. Culture carries out the three functions of mediation, sense-making of situations, and creation of a moral

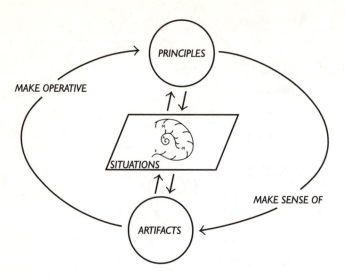

Figure 7 Culture as a device clarifying the ambiguity of everyday situations by means of principles (P) and artifacts (A).

framework for social and individual action. Alan Costall (1995), commenting on Gibson's concept of environmental affordances, observes that

> nature has become artificial and social through a variety of interrelated processes, not all of them unique to the human case . . . Things, surfaces, even animals and plants, have been shaped by human intervention, either deliberately, as in design of implements, or else unconsciously; paths, for example, are created as incidental products of the very activity of walking.
>
> (Costall, 1995: 477)

In everyday experience, people interact with objects and in so doing make them part of the social game. The use of objects cannot then be separated from the care necessary to maintain them in good condition. "Objects do not simply exist, they are maintained. We are justified in taking many things for granted, precisely because someone is accountable for their reliable and safe functioning" (Costall, 1995: 477). The conclusion of this note is that "objects exist within a moral order" – which is just another way of speaking of culture.

7. Education as a cultural process

In the transition from cross-cultural studies on human development to current socio-cultural research on cognition and education, the turning-point, according to Barbara Rogoff and Palbo Chavajay (1995), can be located around 1980. Cross-cultural research from the 1960s until the late 1970s highlighted the role of schooling in forming cognitive differences among children socialized in different cultures (Rogoff, 1981). These researches rejected Piaget's ideas on the development of human intelligence, which presumed that the highest level, that of formal operations, was essentially culture-free. Cross-cultural research showed that the capacity to carry out formal operations was connected with Western-type schooling and Piaget was obliged to recognize that his fourth stage did not indicate a universal step in the development of intelligence but a process depending on its cultural context. Cross-cultural studies did not only discard the idea of a general, all-purpose, decontextualized "mental logic", but also showed that, as regards success in cognitive tests carried out by children in Western and other cultures, familiarity with the objects, operations and words used in the tests was decisive and, to an even greater extent, so was the similarity between the use of the objects required during the tests and the way in which they were currently used in the children's culture. This step opened the way to comprehension of the importance of everyday cognition, i.e., the way in which people usually think in real life when they go shopping or buy a car or try to persuade others to do something. The mental operations people carry out in their everyday lives are far removed from those considered by arithmetic or logic as taught at school; however, they are highly sophisticated operations because they are capable of coping satisfactorily with the ambiguities of real world situations. Schools were advised to pay more attention to people's everyday strategies and to learn from socio-cultural practices (Lave, 1988; Lave and Wenger, 1991).

During the 1980s, cross-cultural research underwent a crisis, due both to its very success – the ubiquity and depth of cultural influence, once recognized, made the use of standardized methods and concepts in different cultural environments questionable – and to the appearance in the Anglo-Saxon world of Vygotsky's socio-historical theory, which offered a sound theoretical framework for the function of mediation carried out by culture. Urie Bronfenbrenner, Mike Cole, Jean Lave, Sylvia Scribner and Barbara Rogoff are among the most representative figures of this socio-cultural *nouvelle vague*, which has profoundly changed studies on cognition and education. Socio-cultural research conceives learning not as a process of transmission of knowledge from an expert to an inexpert person (learning model controlled by an adult) or the acquisition of knowledge (learning model controlled by a child), but as an activity by means of which a community stimulates the acquisition of new competences by its members in ways similar to those used to train apprentices in traditional societies (Rogoff, 1990, 1994, 1995). When school is organized as a community of learners, children are asked to collaborate in a common activity, the relationship focuses on conversation instead of on the sequence "question – answer – assessment", the adult's role is that of guiding the work, distributing responsibility for activities among the children, and of coordinating the flow of interactions occurring in the classroom. Learning in this sense is not an individual performance but a social process. Bruner (1993) objects to the conception of cultural learning as an individual process (Tomasello et al., 1993): he says that one does not learn a culture, one only enters it. Cultural learning is the work of a "community of practices" (Brown et al., 1989; Clancey, 1994) which, while its grown-up members do their tasks, allows the youngest members to acquire the skills necessary to do those tasks themselves. In order to survive, every culture must know how to provide cultural transmission:

> All human societies face cognitive tasks that are beyond the capabilities of any individual member. Even the simplest culture contains more information than could be learned by any individual in a life-time, so the tasks of learning, remembering, and transmitting cultural knowledge are inevitably distributed. The performance of cognitive tasks that exceed individual abilities is always shaped by a social organization of distributed cognition. Doing without a social organization of distributed cognition is not an option.
>
> (Hutchins, 1995: 262)

Studies on everyday cognition, the Theory of Situated Action, and Vygotsky's tradition share this idea, that the transmission of complex abilities is the result of finely tuned cultural processes providing efficient social distribution of knowledge.

A different itinerary towards the cultural dimension is that of Bruner (1990, 1996), who sees the search for meaning as the core of education. Narrations are the places in which sense-making is constructed and negotiated among actors. In stories, we encounter a double landscape, one composed of actors' circumstances and actions and the other of their mental states. When something unexpected happens in the story, the narrator refers to the actors' thoughts or feelings in order to explain it. In this way, the narration makes exceptional occurrences comprehensible, and at the same time reinforces common opinion about what sort of events can be considered normal in a given culture. Both these approaches to the cultural dimension of education are included in this text: Bruner's, which follows the thread linking culture and sense-making, and Rogoff's, which starts from mediation, "cognition in practice" and socially distributed knowledge. The sharp contrast between educational practices aiming at cultural transmission and those aiming at transmitting information is illustrated in Chapters 10 and 11 of this book.

References

Agre, P. (1995) 'The soul gained and lost: artificial intelligence as a philosophical project', *Stanford Humanities Review* 4 (2): 1–19.

Agre, P. (1997) 'Toward a critical technical practice: Lessons learned trying to reform AI', in G.C. Bowker, S.L. Star, W. Turner and L. Gasser (eds), *Social Science, Technical Systems, and Cooperative Work*, Mahwah, NJ; Erlbaum.

Allport, G.W. (1954) *The Nature of Prejudice*, Reading, MA; Addison Wesley.

Antaki, C. (1994) *Explaining and Arguing. The Social Organization of Accounts*, London, Sage.

Atlan, H. (1987) *A Tort et à Raison*, Paris, Seuil.

Bakhtin, M.M. (1981) *The Dialogic Imagination*, Austin, TX, The University of Texas Press.

Bateson, G. (1972) *Steps to an Ecology of Mind*, London, Chandler.

Billig, M. (1987) *Arguing and Thinking: A Rhetorical Approach to Social Psychology*, Cambridge, Cambridge University Press.

Boas, F. (1920) 'The methods of ethnology', *American Anthropologist*, 22: 311–321.

Bond, M.H. and Smith, P.B. (1996) 'Cross-cultural social and organizational psychology', *Annual Review of Psychology*, 47: 205–235.

Borges, J. (1960) *Otras Inquisiciones*, Buenos Aires, Emecé; (1966) *Other Inquisitions*, New York, Washington Square Press.

Brown, J.S., Collins, A. and Duguid, P. (1989) 'Situated cognition and the culture of learning', *Educational Researcher*, 18: 32–42.

Bruner, J. (1990) *Acts of meaning*, Cambridge, MA, Harvard University Press.

Bruner, J. (1993) 'Do we "acquire" culture or vice versa?', *Behavioral and Brain Sciences*, 16: 515–516.

Bruner, J. (1996) *The Culture of Education*, Cambridge, MA, Harvard University Press.

Burke, K. (1957) *The Philosophy of Literary Form*, New York, Vintage Books.

Byron R. (1937 [1992]) *The Road to Oxiana*, London, Penguin.

Cabeza de Vaca, A.N. (1542 [1989]) *Naufragi*, Torino, Einaudi.

Canetti, E. (1964) *Die Stimmen von Marrakesch*, Munchen, Hanser.

Carroll, L. (1865 [1994]) *Alice's Adventures in Wonderland*, London, Penguin.

Carroll, L. (1872 [1984]) *Through the Looking Glass*, London, Penguin.

Chatwin, B. (1987) *The Songlines*, London, Pan.

Ciborra, C. (ed.) (1996) *Groupware and Teamwork*, Chichester, Wiley.

Clancey, W.J. (1994) 'Practice cannot be reduced to theory', in G. Zucc*hermaglio, S. Bagnara and S. Stucky (eds), *Organizational Learning and Technological Change*, Berlin, Springer.

Clancey, W.J. (1997) *Situated Cognition*, Cambridge, Cambridge University Press.

Cole, M. (1990) 'Cultural psychology – a once and future discipline', in J.J. Berman (ed), *Cross-cultural Perspectives – Nebraska Symposium on Motivation 1989*, Lincoln, University of Nebraska Press.

Cole, M. (1995a) 'Culture and cognitive development: from cross-cultural research to creating systems of cultural mediation', *Culture & Psychology*, 1 (1): 25–54.

Cole, M. (1995b) 'Socio-cultural-historical psychology', in J.V. Wertsch, P. del Rio and A. Alvarez (eds), *Sociocultural Studies of Mind*, New York, Cambridge University Press.

Cole, M. (1996) *Cultural psychology – A Once and Future Discipline*, Boston, MA, Harvard University Press.

Cole, M. (1999) 'Cultural psychology: Some general priciples and a concrete example', in Y. Engeström and R. Miettinen (eds), *Perspective on Activity Theory*, Cambridge, Cambridge University Press.

Cole M. and Engeström, Y. (1993) 'A cultural-historical approach to distributed cognition', in G. Salomon (ed.), *Distributed Cognitions*, Cambridge, Cambridge University Press.

Cole, M., Gay J., Glick J.A. and Sharp D.W. (1971) *The Cultural Context of Learning and Thinking*, New York, Basic Books.

Columbus, C. (1493 [1930]) *Selected Documents Illustrating the Four Voyages of Columbus*, London, Hakluyt Society.

Condor, S. and Antaki, C. (1997) 'Social cognition and discourse', in T.A. van Dijk (ed), *Discourse as Structure and Process*, London, Sage.

Cortez, H. (1520 [1963]) *Cartas y Documentos*, Mexico, Porrua.

Costall, A. (1995) 'Socializing affordances', *Theory & Psychology* 5 (4): 467–481.

Defoe, D. (1719 [1972]) *Robinson Crusoe*, Oxford, Oxford University Press.

Del Rio, P. and Alvarez, A. (1995) 'Tossing, praying, and thinking – the changing architectures of mind and agency', in J.V. Wertsch, P. del Rio and A. Alvarez (eds), *Sociocultural Studies of Mind*, New York, Cambridge University Press.

Dixon, R.M.W. (1982) *Where Have all the Adjectives Gone?*, Berlin, De Gruyter.

Donaldson, T. (1996) 'Values in tension: Ethics away from home', *Harvard Business Review*, 74 (5): 48–62.

Dorkenoo, E. (1994) *Cutting the Rose. Female Genital Mutilation*, London, Minority Press.

Drew, P. and Heritage, J.C. (1992) *Talk at Work: Interaction in Institutional Settings*, Cambridge, Cambridge University Press.

Duranti, A. (1997) *Linguistic Anthropology*, Cambridge, Cambridge University Press.

Edwards, D. (1991) 'Categories are for talking: on the cognitive and discursive bases of categorization', *Theory & Psychology* 1: 515–542.

Edwards, D. (1997) *Discourse and Cognition*, London, Sage.

Edwards, D. and Potter, J. (1992) *Discursive Psychology*, London, Sage.

Edwards, D. and Potter, J. (1993) 'Language and causation: a discursive action model of description and attribution', *Psychological Review* 100: 23–41.

Elon, A. (1995) 'Israel's demons', *The New York Review of Books* December 21: 42–46.

Firth, R. (1960) 'A Polynesian aristocrat', in J.B. Casagrande (ed.), *In the Company of Man: Twenty Portraits by Anthropologists*, New York, Harper & Brothers.

Geertz, C. (1973) *The Interpretation of Culture*, New York, Basic Books.

Geertz, C. (1983) *Local Knowledge, Further Essays in Interpretive Anthropology*, New York, Basic Books.

Geertz, C. (1995) *After the Facts: Two Countries, Four Decades, One Anthropologist*, Cambridge, MA, Harvard University Press.

Gergen, K.J. (1973) 'Psychology as history', *Journal of Personality and Social Psychology* 26: 309–320.

Gergen, K.J. (1988) 'If persons are texts', in S.B. Messer, L.A. Sass and R.L. Woolfolk (eds), *Hermeneutics and Psychological Theory*, New Brunswick, NJ, Rutgers University Press.

Gergen, K.J. (1989) 'Social psychology and the wrong revolution', *European Journal of Social Psychology* 19: 436–484.

Gergen, K.J. (1991) *The Saturated Self*, New York, Basic Books.

Gergen, K.J. (1994) *Realities and Relationships – Soundings in Social Construction*, Cambridge, MA, Harvard University Press.

Gergen, K.J. and Gergen M.M. (1983) 'Narratives of the self', in T.R. Sarbin and K.E. Scheibe (eds), *Studies in Social Identity*, New York, Praeger.

Gergen, K.J., Gulerce, A., Lock, A. and Misra, G. (1996) 'Psychological science in cultural context', *American Psychologist* 51: 496–503.

Grassivaro Gallo, P. and Viviani, F. (1992) 'The origin of infibulation in Somalia. An ethological hypothesis', *Ethology and Sociobiology* 13: 253–265.

Greenblatt, S. (1991) *Marvelous Possessions. The Wonder of the New World*, Oxford, Clarendon Press.

Greenfield, P.M. (1997) 'You can't take it with you – why ability assessments don't cross cultures', *American Psychologist* 52: 1115–1124.

Grinker, R.R. (1990) 'Images of denigration', *American Ethnologist* 17: 111–130.

Grinker, R.R. (1994) *Houses in the Rainforest*, Berkeley, University of California Press.

Grossman, D. (1986) *"Ayen" erekh: ahavà*, Tel Aviv, Hoza'at Hakibbutz; 1990, *See under "Love"*, London, Cape.

Gruzinski, S. (1988) *La Colonisation de l' Imaginaire*, Paris, Gallimard; 1993, *The Conquest of Mexico*, Cambridge, Polity Press.

Haddon, A.C. (1901) *Report of the Cambridge Anthropological Expedition to the Torres Straits*, Cambridge, Cambridge University Press.

Harré, R. (1974) 'Blueprint for a new science', in N. Armistead (ed.), *Reconstructing Social Psychology*, Harmondsworth, Pelican.

Helms, L.V. (1882) 'Pioneering in the Far East and journeys to California in 1849 and in the White Sea in 1848', in C. Geertz, *Local Knowledge: Further Essays in Interpretive Anthropology*, New York, Basic Books, 1983.

Hobart, M. (1987) 'Summers' days and salad days: the coming of age of anthropology?', in L. Holy (ed.), *Comparative Anthropology*, Oxford, Blackwell.

Holland, D., Lachicotte, W., Skineer, D. and Cain, C. (1998) *Identity and Agency in Cultural Worlds*, Cambridge, MA, Harvard University Press.

Holyoak, K.J. and Thagard, P. (1995) *Mental Leaps – Analogy in Creative Thought*, Cambridge, MA, The MIT Press.

Hutchins, E. (1995) *Cognition in the Wild*, Cambridge, MA, The MIT Press.

Ishiguro, K. (1989) *The Remains of the Day*, London, Faber and Faber.

Israel, J. and Tajfel, H. (1972) *The Context of Social Psychology. A Critical Assessment*, London, Academic Press.

Jahoda, G. (1992) *Crossroads Between Culture and Mind*, New York, Harvester.

Jahoda, G. (1995) 'The ancestry of a model', *Culture & Psychology* 1 (1): 11–24.

Johnson, M. (1993) *Moral Imagination – Implications of Cognitive Science for Ethics*, Chicago, The University of Chicago Press.

Kearney, M. (1995) 'The local and the global: the anthropology of globalization and transnationalism', *Annual Review of Anthropology* 24: 245–265.

Kling, R. (1994) 'Reading "All about" computerization: how genre conventions shape nonfiction social analysis', *The Information Society* 10 (3): 147–172.

Lakoff, G. (1987) *Women, Fire and Dangerous Things*, Chicago, The University of Chicago Press.

Lakoff, G. and Johnson, M. (1980) *Metaphors We Live By*, Chicago, The University of Chicago Press.

Lave, J. (1988) *Cognition in Practice*, Cambridge, Cambridge University Press.

Lave, J. and Wenger, D. (1991) *Situated Learning*, Cambridge, MA, Harvard University Press.

Lazarus, R.S. (1991) *Emotion and Adaptation*, New York, Oxford University Press.

Leon-Portilla, M. (1964) *El Reverso de la Conquista – Relaciones Aztecas, Mayas y Incas*, Mexico, Mortiz.

Leontiev, A.N. (1978) *Activity, Consciousness, and Personality*, Englewood Cliffs, NJ, Prenctice-Hall.

Levi, P. (1989) *Appendice A: Se Questo è un Uomo*, Torino, Einaudi.

Lewis B. (1995) *Cultures in Conflict: Christians, Muslims and Jews in the Age of Discovery*, New York, Oxford University Press.

Lewis N. (1993) *An Empire of the East*, London, Cape.

Lubek, I. (1997) 'Reflexively recycling social psychology', in T. Ibanez and L. Iniguez (eds), *Critical Social Psychology*, London, Sage.

Luria, A.R. (1979) *The Making of Mind*, Cambridge, MA, Harvard University Press.

Malt, B.C. (1995) 'Category Coherence in Cross-Cultural Perspective, *Cognitive Psychology*, 29: 85–148.

Mantovani, G. (1994) 'Is computer mediated communication intrinsically apt to enhance democracy in organizations?', *Human Relations* 47 (1): 45–62.

Mantovani, G. (1995) 'Virtual reality as a communication environment: consensual hallucination, fiction and possible selves', *Human Relations* 48 (1): 669–683.

Mantovani, G. (1996a) *New Communication Environments*, London, Taylor & Francis.

Mantovani, G. (1996b) 'Social context in HCI: a new framework for mental models, cooperation and communication', *Cognitive Science* 20: 237–269.

Mantovani, G. and Riva, G. (1999) ' "Real" presence: how different ontologies generate different criteria for presence, telepresence, and virtual presence', *Presence – Teleoperators and Virtual Environments* 8 (5): 538–548.

Negroponte, N. (1995) *Being Digital*, London, Hodder & Stoughton.

Neruda, P. (1950) *Canto General*, Mexico, Talleres Graficos de la Nacion.

Norman, D.A. (1992) *Turn Signals are the Facial Expressions of Automobiles*, Reading, MA, Addison-Wesley.

Ochs, E. (1997) 'Narrative', in T.A. van Dijk (ed.), *Discourse as Structure and Process – Volume 1*, London, Sage.

Ochs, E. and Capp, L. (1996) 'Narrating the self', *Annual Review of Anthropology* 25: 19–43.

Oe, K. (1987) 'Natsukashii toshi e no tegami'; 1997 *Gli Anni della Nostalgia*, Milano, Garzanti.

Potter, J. (1996) *Representing Reality: Discourse Rhetoric and Social Construction*, London, Sage.

Potter, J. and Wetherell, M. (1987) *Discourse and Social Psychology. Beyond Attitudes and Behaviour*, London, Sage.

Rogoff, B. (1981), 'Schooling and the development of cognitive skills', in H.C. Triandis and A. Heron (eds), *Advances of Cross-Cultural Psychology – Volume 4*, Rockleigh, NJ, Allyn & Bacon.

Rogoff, B. (1990) *Apprenticeship in Thinking*, New York, Oxford University Press.

Rogoff, B. (1994) 'Developing understanding of the idea of communities of learners', *Mind, Culture and Activity* 1: 209–229.

Rogoff, B. (1995) 'Observing sociocultural activities on three planes: participatory appropriation, guided participation, and apprenticeship', in J.V. Wertsch, P. del Rio and A. Alvarez (eds), *Sociocultural Studies of Mind*, New York, Cambridge University Press.

Rogoff, B. and Chavajay, P. (1995) 'What's become of research on the cultural basis of cognitive development?' *American Psychologist* 50 (10): 859–877.

Rosaldo, M. (1984) 'Toward an anthropology of self and feeling', in R.A. Shweder and R.A. LeVine (eds), *Culture Theory – Essays on Mind, Self, and Emotion*, Cambridge, Cambridge University Press.

Rosaldo, R. (1989) *Culture and Truth. The Remaking of Social Analysis*, Boston, MA, Beacon Press.

Rosch, E. (1978) 'Principles of categorization', in E. Rosch and B. Lloyd (eds), *Cognition and Categorization*, Hillsdale, NJ, Erlbaum.

Sacks, H. (1992) *Lectures on Conversation – Volumes 1 & 2*, Oxford, Blackwell.

Schlegoff, E.A. (1993) 'Conversation Analysis and Socially Shared Cognition', in L.B. Resnick, J.M. Levine and S.D. Teasley (eds), *Perspectives on Socially Shared Cognition*, Washington, DC, American Psychological Association.

Schön D.A. (1979) 'Generative metaphor: a perspective on problem-setting in social policy', in A. Orthony (ed.), *Metaphor and Thought*, Cambridge, Cambridge University Press.

Shore, B. (1996) *Culture in Mind – Cognition, Culture and the Problem of Meaning*, New York, Oxford University Press.

Shweder, R.A. (1991) *Thinking Through Cultures. Expeditions in Cultural Psychology*, Cambridge, MA, Harvard University Press.

Shweder R.A. (1995) 'The confessions of a methodological individualist', *Culture & Psychology* 1 (1): 115–122.

Shweder, R.A. and Sullivan, M. (1990) 'The semiotic person of cultural psychology', in L. Pervin (ed.), *Handbook of Personality*, New York, Guilford.

Shweder, R.A. and Sullivan, M. (1993) 'Cultural psychology: Who needs it?', *Annual Review of Psychology* 44: 497–523.

Slovic, P. (1995) 'The construction of preference', *American Psychologist* 50 (5): 364–371.

Smith, J. (1982) 'The bare facts of the ritual', in *Imagining Religion: From Babylon to Jamestown*, Chicago, The University of Chicago Press.

Soloway, E., Wallace, R. (1997) 'Does the Internet support student inquiry? Don't ask', *Communications of the ACM* 40 (5): 11–16.

Spears, R. (1997) 'Introduction', in T. Ibanez and L. Iniguez (eds), *Critical Social Psychology*, London, Sage.

Spellman, B.A. and Holyoak, K.J. (1992) 'If Saddam is Hitler then who is George Bush? Analogical mapping between systems of social roles', *Journal of Personality and Social Psychology* 62: 913–933.

Sperber, D. (1974) *Le Symbolisme en Géneral*, Paris, Hermann.

Stanner, W.E.H. (1960) 'Durmugam, the Nangiomeri', in J.B. Casagrande (ed), *In the Company of Man. Twenty Portraits of Anthropological Informants*, New York, Harper and Bros.

Tajfel, H. (1972) 'Experiments in a vacuum', in J. Israel, and H. Tajfel (eds), *The Context of Social Psychology: A Critical Assessment*, London, Academic Press.

Tajfel, H. (1981) *Human Groups and Social Categories: Studies in Social Psychology*, Cambridge, Cambridge University Press.

Tajfel, H. and Turner, J.C. (1986) 'The social identity theory of intergroup behaviour', in S. Workell and W.G. Austin (eds), *Psychology of Intergroup Relations*, Chicago, Nelson-Hall.

Todorov, T. (1982) *La Conquete de l' Amérique. La Question de l' Autre*, Paris, Seuil; 1984, *The Conquest of America*, New York, Harper & Row.

Todorov, T. (1996) *L' homme Dépaysé*, Paris, Seuil.

Tomasello, M., Kruger, A.C. and Ratner, H.H. (1993) 'Cultural learning', *Behavioral and Brain Sciences* 16: 495–552.

Triandis, H.C. (1990) 'Cross-cultural studies of individualism and collectivism', in J.J. Berman (ed), *Cross-cultural Perspectives – Nebraska Symposium on Motivation 1989*, Lincoln, University of Nebraska Press.

Tversky, A. and Thaler, R.H. (1990) 'Anomalies: preference reversals', *Journal of Economic Perspectives* 4: 201–211.

Valsiner, J. (1987) *Culture and the Development of Children's Action*, New York, Wiley.

Valsiner, J. (1994) 'Bi-directional cultural transmission and constructive sociogenesis', in R. Maier and W. de Graff (eds), *Mechanisms of Sociogenesis*, New York, Springer.

Valsiner, J. (1998) *The Guided Mind – A Sociogenetic Approach to Personality*, Cambridge, MA, Harvard University Press.

van Dijk, T.A. (1984) *Prejudice in Discourse*, Amsterdam, Benjamin.

van Dijk, T.A. (1987) *Communicating Racism: Ethnic Prejudice in Thought and Talk*, Newbury Park, CA, Sage.

van Dijk, T.A. (1991) *Racism and the Press*, London, Routledge.

van Dijk, T.A. (1993a) *Elite Discourse and Racism*, Newbury Park, CA, Sage.

van Dijk, T.A. (1993b) 'Stories and racism', in D.K. Mumby (ed), *Narrative and Social Control*, Newbury Park, CA, Sage.

van Dijk, T.A. (1997) 'The study of discourse', in T.A. van Dijk (ed), *Discourse as Structure and Process*, London, Sage.

Warburg Spinelli, I. (1990) *Die Dringlichkeit des Mitleids und die Einsamkeit, nein zu sagen. Erinnerungen 1910–1989*, Hamburg, Dollig und Galitz.

Wassmann, J. (1995) 'The final requiem for the omniscient informant? An interdisciplinary approach to everyday cognition', *Culture & Psychology* 1 (2): 167–202.

Weick, K.E. (1990) 'Technology as equivoque: Sensemaking in new technologies', in P.S. Goodman and L.S. Sproull (eds), *Technology and Organizations*, San Francisco, CA, Jossey-Bass.

Weick, K.E. (1995) *Sensemaking in Organizations*, Thousand Oaks, CA, Sage.

Wertsch, J.V. (1985) *Vygotsky and the Social Formation of Mind*, Cambridge, MA, Harvard University Press.

Wertsch, J.V. (1991) *Voices of the Mind*, Cambridge, MA, Harvard University Press.

Wertsch, J.V. (1995) 'Sociocultural research in the copyright age', *Culture & Psychology* 1 (1): 81–102.

Wertsch, J.V., Del Rio, P. and Alvarez, A. (1995) 'Sociocultural studies: history, action, and mediation', in J.V. Wertsch, P. Del Rio and A. Alvarez (eds), *Sociocultural Studies of Mind*, Cambridge, Cambridge University Press.

Wetherell, M. and Potter, J. (1988) 'Discourse analysis and the social psychology of racism', in C. Antaki (ed), *Analysing Everyday Explanations: A Casebook of Methods*, London, Sage.

Wetherell, M. and Potter, J. (1992) *Mapping the Language of Racism: Discourse and the Legitimacy of Exploitation*, Hemel Hempstead, Harvester.

Zhang, J. and Norman, D.A. (1994) 'Representations in distributed cognitive tasks', *Cognitive Science* 18: 87–122.

Index